| DATE | | | |
|---|---|---|---|
| | | | |
| | | | |
| | | | |
| | | | |
| | | | |
| | | | |
| | | | |
| | | | |
| | | | |
| | | | |
| | | | |
| | | | |

# WHERE DID THE TIME GO?

**How to Order:**

Quantity discounts are available from Prima Publishing, P.O. Box 1260KLE, Rocklin, CA 95677; telephone (916) 786-0426. On your letterhead include information concerning the intended use of the books and the number of books you wish to purchase.

# WHERE DID THE TIME GO?
## THE WORKING WOMAN'S GUIDE
## TO CREATIVE TIME MANAGEMENT

Ruth Klein

**Prima Publishing**
P.O. Box 1260KLE
Rocklin, CA 95677
(916) 786-0426

Excerpts from Cathy Guisewite's comic strip "Cathy" reprinted by permission.

Production by Janelle Rohr, Bookman Productions
Copyediting by Toni Murray
Interior design by Judith Levinson
Typography by AeroType, Inc.
Jacket design by The Dunlavey Studio

**Library of Congress Cataloging-in-Publication Data**

Klein, Ruth.
    Where did the time go? / Ruth Klein.
      p. cm.
    Includes index.
    ISBN 1-55958-222-7 : $19.95
      1. Women—United States—Time management.  I. Title.
HQ1221.K54  1992                92-20836
                                           CIP

93  94  95  96  97  RRD  10  9  8  7  6  5  4  3  2  1

Printed in the United States of America

*I dedicate this book to my wonderful husband, Alan, who supported me by his positive attitude, by taking care of the "home front," and by his unconditional love for me; to my daughter, Naomi, whose love and confidence helped me through some tough times; to my oldest son, David, who lovingly reminded me that each day is a new day and should be taken as it comes; and to my youngest son, Daniel, who is a daily reminder of the propriety of the title of this book and a true inspiration to me.*

*This book is also dedicated to my brother, Sherman, whose faith in me kept my confidence up, and to my mom and dad, Genia and Martin, who instilled in me love and an independent spirit that allowed me to develop into the person I am.*

*In addition, I dedicate this book to all the women who have shared a bit of their lives with me through interviews, seminars, and friendship.*

*I am greatly indebted to all of you.*

# CONTENTS

Contents xi

# ACKNOWLEDGMENTS

This book is an effort of many years, and there are some special people who deserve special thanks for helping me bring it to fruition. My agent, Natasha Kern, believed in me and this book and encouraged me to make the book a reality. Thanks to Duane Newcomb, who always made time to talk to me about my progress and made me feel as though I knew what I was doing. Finally, my thanks to Kat and Larry Martin, two great writers who opened their homes to me, shared their writing skills, and supported me during those nerve-wracking days when my proposal was being created.

# INTRODUCTION

Because I grew up with two parents who worked full-time, I learned to become self-sufficient and independent when quite young. My parents are immigrants, having come to America after World War II. They were not familiar with American culture; values; time-pressures; and, most important at the time, games and toys. If my brother and I wanted to play games, we had to develop them ourselves. Since my brother had nice printing, he was in charge of constructing board games. I was in charge of the creative games, like Restaurant, Hollywood, and others I'm sure you haven't heard of.

I also learned that if I wanted to spend more time with my brother, whom I still admire, I needed to learn how to play with miniature cars, basketballs, and Ping-Pong paddles. (Ten years after first learning to play Ping-Pong, I won first place in the local women's division.)

As I grew older, finished school, and got married, I found myself, like most women, taking care of the house, grocery shopping, cooking, raising a family, and working. I became what *Redbook* magazine calls a juggler. I juggled my business, children, home, husband, and all my other activities in a limited time frame.

I found myself uptight and extremely stressed. If I had kept juggling, I probably would have had some sort of breakdown. Instead, I realized that much of my problem stemmed from not properly organizing my time. But when I started looking for help, I found that, though much had been written about time management, almost no authority had addressed the special problems facing working women.

For instance, men rarely have to figure out how to do the wash, keep the house clean, and still work late at the office. The book *The Second Shift* states that the changes in women and the absence of change in men creates a

situation where men simply aren't really helping.[1] These
time-management problems are real and need to be seriously addressed. Time issues not only affect our daily 24
hours, but also the quality of our work, our lives at home,
and our overall health.

This started me on a search to discover how to use my
time more effectively, cut down on the stress and guilt that
comes from having to neglect something or someone, and
still accomplish what I needed to accomplish—every day,
week, and year.

To do this, I read everything I could find on time
management, observed my own life, and interviewed
numerous working women. What I discovered was that the
issue of time tends to be a common denominator in the
lives of all working women. It is also the one thing that
keeps most working women from leading stress-free and
guilt-free lives.

I find that women view time far differently than men.
Women often perceive time as an enemy that prevents
them from getting it all done, all the time. For some reason
society has decided that, even when a woman works, she
is still responsible for making sure that everything gets
done at home—and to this end she never has enough
time. It's true that men also want to accomplish more
in less time, but that nearly always means accomplishing
tasks at work, with their hobbies, or with outside interests at home. Men's concerns rarely include the day-to-
day tasks of running the house and the family. I have
found that this concern that women have for home tasks,
family, and work are at the root of much of their concern
about time.

These special time-pressures cause many working
women to feel overwhelmed, guilty, and stressed. Because
they don't have the time to get everything done, they tend

[1]Hochschild, Arlie, and Anne Machung. *The Second Shift: Inside the Two-
Job Marriage.* New York: Viking, 1989.

to put off those things that are really important to them. Working women usually give top priority to the family or others.

This book is designed to help you balance priorities. In it, I will ask you to decide what you want to accomplish in your life. Then I will offer a number of suggestions to help you manage your time as a working woman (inside or outside the home) so that you can live your life productively and happily 24 hours a day.

One of the problems I found when doing the surveys for this book was that not every working woman had the same objectives. Some wanted to put their entire time emphasis on taking care of the home and children, yet work everything else in. Others weren't quite sure what they wanted, and some wanted to put all their time into their careers.

The study, "The New Diversity: A *Self* Magazine Report on American Women," helped me greatly as I grappled with the matter of women's differing objectives.[2] The study defined several types of women who shared the same priorities in regard to how they wanted to use their time for work, home, and personal activities. This study supported my own view that time management must be powered by personal values—that no one system would be right for every woman. In my work, I simplified the typology presented in the *Self* study. I offer three categories—the Traditional Homemaker, the Transitional Woman, and the Achieving Woman—as labels for discussing distinct attitudes and paths to happiness.

As you read *Where Did the Time Go?* you will be able to see which category you fit into and determine if you are using your time in a way that matches your values and makes you happy. You may be surprised at what you find. For instance, the Traditional Homemaker is happiest when

[2]This study was analyzed in "Transition," *Marketing Insights Magazine,* Fall 1989, p. 27.

she spends about 20% of her time on professional tasks, 50% on home-related tasks, and 30% on personal activities. If you are a Traditional Homemaker and find yourself spending 50% of your time on professional activities, 20% at home, and 30% on personal activities, you may well be chronically unhappy and frustrated. Similarly, an Achieving Woman will find nothing but frustration if she tries to spend 50% of her time on home activities.

The first step in achieving what you want to achieve with your time is to discover what category you fall into and what you want to accomplish. This means developing goals, since goals are the blueprint for change.

In approaching *Where Did the Time Go?* I want you to keep a positive attitude toward change. What does not seem possible to change at first glance may well be just what you need to change. For instance, I recently spoke to a working mom who was picking up her daughter from my son's birthday party. She mentioned how tired she was and how she didn't have the energy to go home and clean the house but that it "had to be done."

Upon direct questioning she told me that her husband doesn't help around the house because he keeps their two cars clean. I pointed out to her that cleaning cars is a weekly job but housework is a daily one. She also realized, however, that she wasn't going to get extra help from him, so she would have to deal with the problem herself.

I suggested that she consider having a cleaning service come in once a week. She protested: Not only could they not afford a cleaning service, but her husband would consider it out of the question. In cases like this I feel it is important to keep a positive attitude toward change. I realize that a lot of women wouldn't consider a cleaning service, but what about a house helper? Perhaps she could trade off for help with a neighbor or friend or maybe she could hire a teenager a few hours a week. Either one of these alternatives would solve a lot of problems.

I also want you to stay flexible and open to new ideas as you read *Where Did the Time Go?* Flexibility means maintaining an internal feeling that everything will work and using whatever method you find necessary to make it work. You may think you can't change something as basic as the time you spend taking care of the children or cleaning the house. But consider what you and your friends have already done. Remember back a few years, when eating "healthy" wasn't even thought of. Many women have made basic changes, and today they are eating more fruit and vegetables, serving balanced meals, and eating a low-fat cholesterol-free diet. If you and others can make basic changes like these, you can also make the changes that will free you from anxiety and guilt and give you a chance to spend your time in those activities that mean the most to you.

A mathematical equation may equal 8. But there are several ways to reach that number: 4 plus 4, 5 plus 3, 2 plus 6, 8 plus 0, and 7 plus 1. They are all correct; it is the choice of which to use that is different. Throughout *Where Did the Time Go?* I will offer you a number of choices to solve individual time problems. To get the most out of the book, you must stay flexible. Don't reject any solution out of hand; consider all of them and pick those you think might work.

Finally, *Where Did the Time Go?* will not do you a bit of good if you read it and then put it back on the shelf. This is an *action* book. Its purpose is to change your life. Nothing, however, will happen unless you take action. Mark some of the suggestions you want to try as you go through the book. When finished, go back and actually try them. In addition, I suggest you consider this a reference book that you refer to over and over.

This book, *Where Did the Time Go?*, encourages you to open your mind and attitude to new ideas and tactics. Feel free to think about them and to modify them. But, whatever you do, pinpoint which group of women you fall into, then decide on the changes you want to make, then *make them*. Remember, without action, nothing at all can happen.

Few women would say that they have achieved time equality at work, at home, or in their personal activities. *Where Did the Time Go?* gives examples of how to balance time. I believe it can help you create a future filled with a new perception of time, a positive attitude toward defining priorities, and a more flexible schedule filled with fresh possibilities. Enjoy!

# 1

# HOW TO MAKE TIME FOR THE TIME OF YOUR LIFE

You've seen her in magazines: Superwoman. She's wearing beautiful, expensive clothes and not one hair is out of place. She's smiling as she holds a briefcase in one hand and her three-year-old daughter in the other. You've seen her on television, where you could swear that her clothes had just arrived straight from the cleaners after being worn by a top-notch, well-endowed model. She walks into a clean, two-story organized home where the children are happy to see mom and dinner will be prepared within minutes.

A more realistic scenario: Diane Keaton's face fills the screen and we see a woman touched by anguish. Her sensitive features contort with pain, causing a shudder of compassion to ripple through the audience. Is this woman facing political ruin or untimely death? Hardly. In this poignant scene from *Baby Boom*, Keaton must make the wrenching choice between meeting with her star client or babysitting a newborn. As a seasoned executive but inexperienced full-time mom, her dilemma is excruciating.

For most working mothers, Keaton's situation is business as usual. Like Keaton's character, they are fighting a losing battle to juggle the thousand and one tasks

1

demanded by job, home, children, husband, friends, and family.

A woman who signed her name "Tired in Texas" summarized the problem in a letter to Ann Landers:

> I put in 40 hours a week downtown and just as many at home. . . . My job as a supervisor is stressful. The demands on me are awesome. Everyone wants something. When I come home, I must prepare supper, clean the house, wash clothes, pick up the kids from their daily activities, help with homework, and see that they are bathed and put to bed. By then I'm dead tired. And each day is busier than the day before. I'm totally shot and feel as if I'm sinking into quicksand. My body says rest, but my mind says get ready for tomorrow. And the real problem is that there isn't enough time to do it all.

This story is typical of working women all across the globe. Most women work out of necessity. Some work so that the family can enjoy niceties, such as a bigger home or an extended family vacation. The problem for most, however, is that the time crunch is killing women physically and emotionally.

What these women want most is the time to handle, without always rushing, all the tasks they deem necessary. The need for time management comes as no surprise to women, who have traditionally been the ones who alter their schedules to accommodate daily activities, errands, and special projects. Men, traditionally, have not had this burden. As Gloria Steinem said several years ago in an interview, "I have yet to hear a man ask for advice on how to combine the time for marriage and a career." And yet people who teach time management expect working women to allocate their time in the same way a working man does. Stated simply, it doesn't work that way.

Women, at all ages, enter or leave the job market; change careers; have children; marry or remarry; start, complete, or add to their educations; run their own busi-

nesses; and more. Many of these varied roles are simul-
taneous, and the result is a *severe time crunch.*

## ESTABLISHING YOUR OWN PERSONAL MOTIVATIONAL LIFESTYLE

As a working woman, you have surely felt the crunch: Meeting the needs of your job and your family threatens to take
all your time; with no time for yourself, you may feel as if
you are about to disappear altogether. How can you resolve
conflicting demands and maintain some sense of personal
peace? The first step is to define how you want to allot
your energy. Let your own values determine how you balance work, family, and personal time and then develop a
lifestyle that reflects your priorities. Only by incorporating
your own values can you maintain a lifestyle that will seem
fulfilling to you and motivate you to grow as an individual.

A study published in *Self* magazine defined seven such
lifestyles, which the study called Personal Motivational
Lifestyles. Each one reflects the values of a certain type
of woman. My own experience in working with women's
time-management issues led me to simplify the *Self* model
by distinguishing three categories. By choosing the category that best reflects your values and then restructuring
your schedule according to the time-allotment percentages
that accompany each category, I feel confident that you
can improve the quality of your life.

The three categories of women are the Traditional
Homemaker, the Transitional Woman, and the Achiever.
See which one best reflects your views and values.

### The Traditional Homemaker: "I Do Have a Career!"

Most Traditional Homemakers plan their lives around
marriage and family, and they always wanted to be

mothers. For these women, caring for home and family takes priority. Today, when most families need two pay-checks to survive, 65% of Traditional Homemakers are employed, 35% of them full-time. Two thirds of the women working full-time would rather stay at home. However, most do not see themselves as full-time homemakers for the rest of their lives. Three fifths of the Traditional Homemakers who are not working currently plan to return to work when their children start school.

For Traditional Homemakers, work outside the home is a 9-to-5 job, not a career. Many of these women feel that the desire to have it all is unrealistic. They believe a woman can't be her best as both a mother and a career woman. Their sense of accomplishment comes from taking care of their home and raising a family. Their traditional values and attitudes lead them to believe that the hus-band's job is more important than the wife's. Because of the consistency between their attitudes and lifestyle, these women seem to be happy. Their good feelings come from knowing that they won't always be at home. Many feel that a new life will begin for them in later years. They feel they have control over their lives, health, and well-being. All, however, believe they need extra time to do everything they want to do, both inside and outside the home.

Many of the women who stay home or work part-time feel that society as a whole does not take them seriously or see them as being as competent as career women. This is especially true for traditional women who worked—who were career women, in fact—but then opted to stay at home to raise their families. They do not want to be looked down on because they are "only housewives." Traditional Homemakers, in their view, do a very worth-while job by taking care of home and family. They view the transitions from work force to home to work force as career changes.

## The Transitional Woman: "I Feel Trapped."

These women have their hearts in neither their work nor their homes. Most Transitional Women are married and many work outside their homes. Only 28% stay at home full-time. A large percentage are forced to work because of economic pressures. Many are employed in jobs they don't particularly like. This in itself creates a strain, and the strain is intensified by the pressure of having to cope with home and work and the guilt of having to neglect the family.

Women in this group lack a feeling of control. They are traditional in their values and attitudes, but they feel forced into working. As temporary "escapes," they tend to be impulsive spenders, watch a lot of television, read magazines for guidance, and change hair and makeup regularly. These stress reducers, when used in excess, only cause more stress in their lives. Over 50% of Transitional Women live from paycheck to paycheck.

Because they perceive that they lack control, women in this group tend to lack confidence in their own ability to find solutions to their conflict. Transitional Women need consistent doses of support and information to help them make life choices. These women haven't decided whether to focus on homemaking or their career. They feel extremely ambivalent.

## The Achievers: "Of Course I Can."

Women who are Achievers are career-centered. They put their hearts and souls into their work. If asked to chair an event, be on a committee, or accept a new assignment or client, these are the women who say "Of course I can." These women find themselves overcommitted, overwhelmed, and overworked. Their greatest fear is loss of

control—professionally, personally, and at home. They feel
that, if their juggling act misses a beat, then everything
will come crashing down.

Yet 85% feel that their lives work well. Both the Achievers and the Traditional Homemakers find consistency
between their values, attitudes, and lifestyles. Of all the
groups, the Achievers rate themselves the highest on self-
confidence. However, the serious time pressures they face
cause them frustration, anxiety, and conflict.

Achievers do not believe, as the Traditional Homemakers do, that the home is the center of life. Rather, they
view their homes as an expression of who they are and
as a refuge from their busy schedules.

Over 64% of Achievers feel they could live comfortably
on their own salary. They tend to be extremely self-reliant
and independent in a relationship. Because they are fierce-
ly independent and financially secure, they tend to leave
a bad marriage sooner than women in the other groups.
In spite of the high percentage of failed marriages among
Achievers, family is important to them. But their strongest
sense of competence and accomplishment comes from
their careers.

More than any other group, the Achievers would like
to start their own businesses, if they had the money.

## GIVE YOURSELF PERMISSION TO
## LIVE THE LIFE YOU WANT

When children are young, we teach them to ask permission to do things and go places. Many women have inter-
nalized the childhood requirement for asking permission.
They think they must ask before they get a job; change
careers; go on an out-of-town business trip; leave for a vacation with a boyfriend, husband, or girlfriend; or take time
for themselves.

To make lifestyle changes, women must learn to give permission to themselves and then turn "permission to . . . " statements into formal action. Setting goals is one of the best ways to give yourself permission, lay the groundwork for your ideas, and turn a desire for change into action.

## Set Goals

Achieving goals takes thought and effort. The *American Heritage Dictionary* says that a goal is (1) a desired result or purpose, an objective; (2) the finish line of a race; (3) in certain sports, a structure or area into which players must propel the ball or puck in order to score.

*Webster's New World Thesaurus* offers other words to replace *goal*: *object, aim,* and *intent.* Goals offer us a way to aim toward our desires and give us a way to grant ourselves permission to do what we need to do.

Goals are a way to turn your desires and intent into meaningful results and define your purpose. To set a goal, you must determine what you really want out of your 24 hours—what you want for you and your family, at work, and in your love relationships. Women spend more time thinking about the weekly grocery and errand list than thinking about what really counts in life.

To set your goals, follow these steps:

1. Start a goal sheet with three headings: "General Goals (Permission to . . .)," "Motivations," and "Specifics."
2. List five general goals—five things you want out of life.
3. Write down your motivations; ask yourself *why* you want each goal. A good way to do this is to talk into a tape recorder about your goals and why you think you want them. When you play the tape back and

listen, the motivations behind your choices may become clear.

4. Under the heading "Specifics," list *how* you can reach your goals. Be creative, brainstorm.

5. Start now!

Most women have no trouble stating general goals, such as saving more money, having nicer or cleaner homes, taking more vacations, or getting a good job. Writing down general goals such as these is the first step in the right direction. Writing down your goals increases your likelihood of achieving them. Seeing your goals in print helps you organize your priorities and reinforces your commitment. In addition, it activates your subconscious in regard to finding ways to reach your goals.

Once you have written down general goals (which also serve as permission to do what you want), write down your motivations for these goals, and then note specifically how you are going to reach them. Jenny, a pharmacist, listed her five major goals: to make more money, take vacations, lose weight, stay healthy, and find a lover. After discussing these general goals, she discovered that she wanted and needed to give herself permission to make more money so that she could have a weekly housekeeper and buy more clothes. She discovered that she needed to give herself permission to go on vacations so that she could get away from the stress at her job, give herself permission to lose weight so she could feel better about her body and feel more sexually comfortable with men, give herself permission to stay healthy in order to keep up her busy schedule, and give herself permission to find a lover to share and discuss her thoughts and fears.

Jenny now had general goals ("permission to . . ." statements) and the motivations behind them. At this point she needed to fill in how she would achieve her goals.

Jenny's goal sheet looked like this:

**GOAL SHEET**

| General Goals (Permission to . . . ) | Motivations | Specifics |
|---|---|---|
| Make more money | Cleaner house | Save $50 out of each paycheck<br>Hire a housekeeper |
|  | Expensive-looking clothes | Shop sales at quality clothing stores |
| Take vacations | Relief of work-related stress | Go to bed early on Friday nights<br>Enjoy Saturday breakfasts alone |
| Lose weight | Feel better about my body | Start a diet<br>Lose 17 pounds |
| Stay healthy | Ability to accomplish all the activities on my busy schedule | Walk 3 times a week (25 minutes before work)<br>Walk at lunch<br>Bring sack lunch from home |
| Find a lover | A man to share my life | Feel good about myself sexually<br>Indulge in new, sexy undergarments<br>Join a singles group |

## SET ASIDE ONE HOUR A DAY

Just as physical exercise is important for keeping physically fit, mental exercise is important for keeping mentally fit. We all know that everyone has 24 hours in a day, but the way we *use* and *perceive* our 24 hours either stresses us out or rejuvenates us.

Most women have heard the saying "An apple a day keeps the doctor away." The updated version for working women is "One hour of personal time a day keeps the time crunch away." We have approximately 6,000 waking hours in a year. About 2,000 are used on working 8-hour days. That leaves 4,000 discretionary hours left (including sleep time).

Certainly you can find seven hours a week to sit quietly and think. Set aside one hour a day—preferably the same time each day, to establish habit—and *just think*. Think of ten ways to improve an activity, a relationship, a belief system, or anything else you find yourself worrying about. Write your ideas down on a legal pad. You do not have to resolve the situation at that moment. Just think and organize your thoughts. You may want to walk and exercise while you're thinking.

You will find that each idea triggers a new idea. This is what happens if you feel comfortable and not pressed for time—your mind wanders. You will find yourself thinking creatively. Most women do not take the time to think creatively about a situation or activity; they are pushed, by others or themselves, into making a decision or solving a problem immediately.

Everything you need to make a decision, change a belief system, or improve a relationship is within your grasp if only you think constructively about it.

## THINK, DON'T WORRY

Most women tend to worry, rather than think, about situations. A lot of this worrying comes from the feeling that women need to make the "right" or "perfect" choice. Remember, however, perfection is not real. Trying to achieve it will stall your creative process. Avoid trying to achieve perfection; just think clearly. If you think chaos, you get chaos. If you think of staying calm and making the best decision at the time, you will stay calm and chances are good that you will make a wise decision. *You are what you think!*

Someone said that 50% of the time we worry about things that never happen, 30% of the time we worry about things that have passed, 12% of the time about health issues, and only 8% of the time about real problems. Of the real problems, half of them we can solve and the other half, we can't. This means we spend 96% of our time on unnecessary worry.

The comic strip "Cathy" said it best:

> Oh, Irving . . . I'm sorry! I've been worrying about myself and ignoring you!
>
> Oh, Charlene . . . I'm sorry! I've been worrying about Irving and ignoring you!
>
> Oh, Electra . . . I'm sorry! I've been worrying about Charlene and ignoring you!
>
> Oh, Mom . . . I'm sorry! I've been worrying about Electra and ignoring you!
>
> Oh, Dad . . . I'm sorry! I've been worrying about Mom and ignoring you!
>
> *(Pant, Pant, Pant, Pant)*
>
> Oh, Self . . . I'm sorry! I've been worrying about everyone else and ignoring you!
>
> HERE WE GO AGAIN . . .

## IMPORTANT POINTS TO REMEMBER

It is important to establish your own Personal Motivational Lifestyle. The lifestyle models this book presents are the Traditional Homemaker, who is family-centered; the Transitional Woman, who may not be fulfilled by her job and feels guilty about the time it takes from her family; and the Achieving Woman, who is career-centered.

To know what you want in life, you must develop goals. In addition, you need to give yourself permission to reach these goals. When developing your goals, remember to be specific. The more specific you are, the easier it will be to achieve what you want out of life.

# 2

# WHERE TO PUT YOUR TIME EMPHASIS

A working woman's time is divided into professional, personal, and home time. However, *how* a woman divides her time should depend primarily on what motivates her. Once the working woman identifies her Personal Motivational Lifestyle (see Chapter 1), she then needs to take stock of how much time she allots to each of these areas and compare her tally to what her motivational lifestyle dictates. If an Achiever puts the major emphasis on the home while her real interest and motivation is work, then the result is stress and unhappiness.

## DISTINGUISHING PROFESSIONAL, HOME, AND PERSONAL TIME

This section will elaborate on the motivational lifestyles described in Chapter 1, so you can see the time allotments that each type of woman tends to feel satisfied with.

The Traditional Homemaker's primary time emphasis is in the home. Traditional Homemakers see themselves as managers of the home and want to be valued for this.

They derive self-confidence from their role as home manager, but they are dependent on positive reinforcement from family and friends. Traditional Homemakers feel that taking time out for themselves is selfish, that they must keep busy with the cleaning, wash, or children to make everything work in time.

A statement from Nancy, a homemaker and substitute teacher, typifies the homemaker's view: "I'm happiest when I'm home playing with my kids. I like substitute teaching because it leaves me time to spend with my children. I'd hate to leave the kids every day—they need me at home."

According to informal surveys conducted by The Marketing Source of Bakersfield, California, most Traditional Homemakers would like to spend 50% of their time at home, taking care of the house or children; 30% on personal activities, such as shopping, hobbies, or lunch with friends; and 20% on professional activities, such as working part-time at an office to supplement family income.

The Transitional Woman's time is split between her professional and home lives. She is torn: Her value system says that women need to take care of the home first and then work if necessary. The Transitional Woman's inability to fulfill the traditional female role makes her dependent on others for satisfaction and happiness. In addition, compared to Traditional Homemakers and Achieving Women, Transitional Women are usually less satisfied with their relationships. This group needs to know that positive changes are possible and that they deserve the good things in life. They need to learn that they have choices.

Elaine, an executive secretary who is a Transitional Woman, feels hurried all the time. "I enjoy the people I work with, clothes hunting, and getting my very own paycheck...but some days I hate to leave my little baby and a messy house."

Most Transitional Women like to spend 35% of their time at home, 35% of their time working, and 30% of their time on personal activities.

The Achieving Woman's primary time emphasis is in her professional life. She derives self-confidence and a feeling of control from her career. Without a career, most of these women feel they have no purpose, even though they may have a family. Her strongest needs are the need to succeed and the need for independence. She is constantly on the go, always trying to make situations better, events bigger, or develop new ideas. She wants to know how and where to go to get something done.

Janet, an accountant, loves her career. "I look forward to going to the office. In fact, sometimes I feel a little guilty that I enjoy my career so much. Some Saturdays I prefer to work at the office instead of staying home."

A typical Achieving Woman wants to spend 50% of her time engaged in professional activity. She would like to spend 25% of her time on personal activities, and 25% of her time or less at home. She tries to cut her home chores by assigning some tasks to other family members, leaning heavily on convenience or prepared foods, or by hiring part-time help in the house when possible.

## DETERMINING HOW TO DIVIDE YOUR TIME

In this section, you will determine your present time emphasis by listing the time spent on all activities, totaling the time spent by category, and then entering the totals in the chart on page 16.

Begin by listing, on a blank sheet of paper, all the activities you performed that day. Then, beside each activity, write the time you spent doing it. Round off your time to the nearest hour—the total for each day will not add up to exactly 24 hours. Circle all work times in yellow, home times in green, and personal times in red. Add all the times circled in the same color, and write each total in the appropriate column of the chart. Determine your total time by category for each day for two weeks.

|              | *Professional Time* | *Home Time* | *Personal Time* |
|--------------|---------------------|-------------|-----------------|
| Monday       |                     |             |                 |
| Tuesday      |                     |             |                 |
| Wednesday    |                     |             |                 |
| Thursday     |                     |             |                 |
| Friday       |                     |             |                 |
| Saturday     |                     |             |                 |
| Sunday       |                     |             |                 |
|              |                     |             |                 |
| Monday       |                     |             |                 |
| Tuesday      |                     |             |                 |
| Wednesday    |                     |             |                 |
| Thursday     |                     |             |                 |
| Friday       |                     |             |                 |
| Saturday     |                     |             |                 |
| Sunday       |                     |             |                 |
|              |                     |             |                 |
| *Totals*     |                     |             |                 |

For example, Sheila works from 8:00 A.M. to 5:00 P.M. every day, with one hour for lunch. She draws a yellow circle around the amount of time she spent at work. If she runs errands at lunch, that hour is considered home time. She circles the "home" total in green. If she takes her lunch hour with a friend, has her hair trimmed, or shops for clothes, the time is personal time; she circles the "personal" total in red.

Preparing dinner, washing dishes, or putting the children to bed is home time. Reading, watching television, or going to the movies is personal time. If, however, she goes to the movies just for the children, then the activity is considered home time.

You will not only see where you are spending your time, but more important, you will be able to decide if your time emphasis is in balance with your motivational lifestyle. You will know you are balanced when you feel peace within, rather than constant turmoil.

When finished, decide what percentage of time you have invested in professional, home, and personal time. Then compare your time with the averages for each type of woman. For instance, suppose you're a Transitional Woman who spends 60% of her time at work, 20% at home, and 20% in personal activities. Compared to the typical allotments for a Transitional Woman—35% professional, 35% home, and 30% personal—your schedule is out of balance. You probably feel the strain it is imposing on you.

You are "wasting time" if your time emphasis is not consistent with your motivational lifestyle. This inconsistency brings general anxiety; fatigue; and time tension, which is an intrusive concern about having the time to get things done.

The standard of 30% personal time may seem overindulgent, selfish, or not possible. Look at the reality, however: After you subtract 7 hours from 24 for sleeping and 12 hours for professional and home activities, you have approximately 5 hours left daily for personal activities. In the remainder of this book, you will learn how to capture these hours.

## How to Achieve the Balance

You have just learned where the different types of women usually feel comfortable putting their time emphasis. Now you'll look at a few examples to see how time use and lifestyle can be mismatched.

## THE TRADITIONAL HOMEMAKER

**Situation**   Sylvia, a Traditional Homemaker, volunteered over 20 hours a week outside her home. "I stay at home and volunteer at my daughter's school, in organizations, and do the books for our family business. The more I do, the more I'm 'volunteered' to do. I'm away from the family on the average of two nights a week and most mornings. I constantly try to find time to do the things I need and want to do—gardening, making crafts, and taking care of the family. I feel like I'm ready to snap."

**Time Mismatch**   Sylvia is a Traditional Homemaker, but she spends 50% of her time outside the home, volunteering. According to her Personal Motivational Lifestyle, she needs to spend 50% at home, 30% on personal activities, and 20% on outside work.

**Time Balance**   Sylvia needs to say no and reprogram her schedule.

**Time Interpretation**   Here is what she had to say after she made the necessary changes: "I chose the one organization I enjoyed most and only volunteer five hours a week, during the day. I started a small vegetable garden with zucchini, tomatoes, and peppers. I still don't have all the time I need to do what I want, but I don't feel like I'm ready to snap, either."

Sylvia changed her time emphasis to reflect her motivational lifestyle, Traditional Homemaker. By combining her personal interest in gardening with her home interest in cooking, she balanced home and personal time. By choosing only one volunteer organization, she was able to spend her "work" time in a way she thought important, freeing her to do other activities consistent with her lifestyle.

**Situation**   Liz, a Traditional Homemaker, works 24 hours outside her home each week. "I work part-time so that our family can have a few extras . . . summer camp for the girls, and nice clothing for the children. By the time I come home and do everything that's needed, I feel anxious and crabby."

**Time Mismatch**   Liz is a Traditional Homemaker, but she spends over 50% of her time outside her home and less than 20% in her home. She needs to reverse these two time allotments.

**Time Balance**   Liz needs to work fewer hours in her present job or find a position that will allow her to work part-time at home. Many jobs fit nicely into this pattern— typing, bookkeeping, proofreading, and design work.

Here is Liz's explanation of the changes she eventually made: "I asked my boss to let me do some bookkeeping at home. We worked out a plan so that I can do this one day a week. I'm able to take on bookkeeping for two new clients now, since I don't waste my time getting prepared in the morning, taking a 30-minute lunch break, or driving to and from work. I keep the same child-care schedule, but get a lot more done."

**Time Interpretation**   Liz changed her time emphasis to reflect her motivational lifestyle, Traditional Homemaker. By combining her part-time job with slightly more responsibility and staying home one day a week to work, she increased her time emphasis in the home while actually increasing what she accomplished for her employer.

### THE TRANSITIONAL WOMAN

**Situation**   Lillian, a Transitional Woman, works constantly and relies on babysitters to watch the children. "I am spending money for someone else to get to know my children while I work. When I have any time at home, I'm too busy washing and cleaning to share any good family time. I'm always rushing and fitting in errands."

**Time Mismatch**   After charting Lillian's schedule, she found that she was spending 45% of her time at work and work-related activities, 35% of her time at home, and 20% of her time on personal activities.

**Time Balance**   Lillian must find a way to spend less time on the job and more time with her family.

**Time Interpretation**   Lillian's boss would not accept flex-time. So she changed to a job that allowed her to keep a flexible schedule, even though the new job paid less. "I couldn't keep up the pace. Even though I make less money, I don't need to use the sitter as much. I've worked a deal out with my neighbor—I take care of her little boy Saturday mornings, and she watches my daughter Wednesday evenings, when my husband and I go to a movie. I pay a neighborhood teen to iron twice a week. During 'iron' time, the family sits at the kitchen table talking, with the television off and the answering machine on. So far, it works out well."

**Situation**   Karen, a Transitional Woman, works all day long. She picks up items around the house in the morning as time allows; works at her full-time job; and comes home, prepares dinner, and continues to straighten the house. "I feel like I'm a walking and talking cleaner-upper. I'm always picking up toys, wrappers, lint, shoes, and other stuff. I need *help* in the house."

**Time Mismatch**   Through charting her time, Karen found that she was spending 50% of her time at work and 50% of her time at home cleaning up. She had no time for personal activities.

**Time Balance**   Karen must decrease the time she spends on housework by hiring help, asking her family for help, or changing her standards.

**Time Interpretation**   Karen delegated some household responsibilities to other family members. She could not afford outside cleaning help, so she turned for help within the household. "I am responsible for the kitchen, my ten-year-old takes the family room, the six-year-old takes the most-used bathroom, and my boyfriend takes our bedroom. I tell them how much it helps and how I have more time for them. I didn't know if it was going to work at first, but the more time I spent with them, the more they made the effort."

## THE ACHIEVING WOMAN

**Situation**   Janie, an Achieving Woman, does not spend what she thinks is enough time at work; this causes her stress. "My mother needs more health care since my dad passed away. I take her to most of her doctor appointments, testing, and such. I have a demanding work schedule that I can't keep up with. I have to come up with something, but don't want to give up my job or sacrifice my mom's health."

**Time Mismatch**   Janie spends 40% of her time at work, 45% of her time at home and with her mom, and 15% of her time on personal activities.

**Time Balance**   Janie must find a way to delegate her mother's care, work more efficiently, or do both.

**Time Interpretation**   "I asked my boss of eight years if I could work at home one day a week. She was not in favor of the idea at first. I explained to her that I would not need to take as much sick leave with this new schedule. We tried it, and it worked. I spend five hours on Wednesdays with Mom. It gives me two days, Monday and Tuesday, to get involved in work and two days, Thursday and Friday, to complete what I've started. I check up on Mom during lunch or after work on the other days. I have a college student come in the afternoons to provide companionship for her."

By negotiating a flexible work schedule with her boss to suit work and her mom, Janie feels that she has more control over work and her mother's care. She takes less sick leave and is able to concentrate more fully on work when she is there.

**Situation**    Louise, an Achieving Woman, is spending most of her waking hours with work-related activities. "I started waking up at 5:00 A.M., going for a walk (on the days I thought I could spare 30 minutes), scheduling business breakfasts at 7:00 or 7:30, and then getting to the office by 8:30. I would come home around 6:30 and plop down. I forced myself to stay up until 11:30 so that I could spend time talking to my husband, who was watching the news on TV. I probably would have kept this up, but I came down with an inner-ear infection. This caused me to lose my equilibrium and *forced* me to take it easy."

**Time Mismatch**    Louise found that she was spending 65% of her time at work or work-related activities, 20% at home, and 15% in personal areas.

**Time Balance**    To decrease the number of hours she spends on her career and to preserve her health, Louise must find a way to work more efficiently or take on fewer projects.

**Time Interpretation**    "I realized that my work was getting done but that I wasn't creating new projects as rapidly. I started focusing on one project at a time, rather than several at once, putting all my effort into one area. My husband and I set up time to talk before the news. I went to bed earlier, slept in later, and made only one early-morning business breakfast a week. It has been almost seven months since I last lost my equilibrium, and I hope to keep it that way. I now feel more in control of my life at work and at home. The doctor wants me to spend more time on myself relaxing. . . . That's my next project."

As you review your own time allotment, remember: Everything you need to make a decision, change a belief system, improve a relationship, or re-divide time is within your grasp *if only you take the time to think constructively about it.*

## FINDING YOUR PEAK TIME

Imagine that each daily square on the calendar is divided into four parts: morning, afternoon, late afternoon, and evening. Until you train your mind's eye to automatically separate the day into four parts, manually draw in three dotted lines to differentiate the sections.

If you have high energy during the morning, plan to do your "brain work" during this "high-energy" time. For you and most women, mornings are the worst time to have meetings; instead, schedule concentration activities during morning hours. Place or return phone calls around 11:30 A.M.

During the lunch hour, give yourself permission to hit a few balls against a wall (playing tennis well is not necessary), take an aerobics class, window-shop, or read for pleasure at a park or cafe. Plan Fridays as business-lunch days. Remember to be flexible. For example, you do not need to stay the entire hour of aerobics. Health experts agree that 20 minutes of aerobic activity is productive (and much better than nothing). You may want to exercise during the lunch hour two or three times a week. During the other lunch hours, you may want to do errands, attend a club meeting, or schedule a business lunch. Remember, be flexible!

If your high-energy time is in the afternoon, this is a good time to start major projects. Do not, however, start a major project and think it will be finished by the end of the day. To do so would be setting yourself up to feel overwhelmed. Plan for in-office time the morning after you start a new project.

Late afternoon is ideal for starting a new project, if late afternoon is your high-energy time. If not, it is an excellent time for placing or returning calls. Late afternoon is also a good time for "morning" people to follow up, read, analyze computer printouts, or write correspondence.

During the evening you might plan to attend a class once or twice a week; do errands one evening a week, have a personal-needs night; stay late at the office; or enjoy a weekly family night, depending on your professional, home, or personal requirements. Remember to be flexible.

Dividing the day not only allows you to see how and where you are spending your time, but it helps you to get going when you're at peak energy. You can see if you're spending your high-energy times in long, drawn-out meetings; in running errands; in accomplishing trivial things; or in putting out fires.

## MATCHING NEEDS AND MOTIVATIONAL LIFESTYLES: TIME TIPS

The need to expand time in a particular segment of your life may be chronic or it may arise in special situations only. Whatever the case, the tips that follow can be useful for all types of women.

### Tips for Expanding Professional Time

The two tips of expanding professional time include a way to share burdens and a way to use time more effectively by organizing it better.

**The SWAT Team**  The SWAT team is a tool for managing both work time and home time, and it is uniquely adapted to the working woman. (Chapter 4, "The Big Glitch," talks about how to develop a SWAT team.) In effect, it helps a working mother be in two places at once by recruiting a group of other women who will fill in for her in many ways. A SWAT team can take the children to the dentist while the working woman performs an essential work task or, conversely, fill in at work while the working mom takes care of a sick child or herself.

The Traditional Homemaker needs to use this tactic if there is an emergency or some kind of deadline approaching. This is also helpful if mom wants to spend some special time with a newborn or other children individually.

The Transitional Woman may think a SWAT team is a good idea, but she may doubt she will find women who will participate. If she looks hard enough, however, a SWAT team emerges.

The Achieving Woman invented this concept. Achieving Women would not be able to enjoy their careers as much if various child-care options were not available. They are always interested in new SWAT team ideas.

**The Month-at-a-Glance Calendar**  A month-at-a-glance calendar is a must. It virtually displays project due dates and reminders about letters to write, appointments to keep, and home and personal commitments that may cut into work time. This smooths out the week and month, and prevents overcommitment during heavily scheduled weeks. Chapter 7, "Taking Control of Your Schedule," details the use of the month-at-a-glance calendar.

The Traditional Homemaker finds the month-at-a-glance calendar helpful in all areas of her life.

The Transitional Woman finds the calendar helpful once she decides to purchase it. It helps her visualize her cluttered schedule.

The Achieving Woman finds she can't live without a month-at-a-glance calendar, once she has started using it.

## Tips for Expanding Home Time

Management of home time constitutes a serious problem. Yet, with a little ingenuity and a few tips, working women can learn to handle most home chores in much less time.

**The Mini–Office-Kitchen**   Women, unlike men, spend hours in the car taking and picking up and running other home-related errands. One time-saver that works especially well is the mini–office-kitchen car trunk, which is an office- and home-supply store on wheels. As Chapter 16 will discuss, if you have supplies with you, you can work anywhere and save many trips to your home, the office, or the store. You can use the trunk of your car to store paper clips, stapler, folders, scratch paper, newsletters, and other items you need repeatedly. Whether or not you have children, having healthful snacks and drinks in the trunk can be a time-saver in the face of a road delay. Keeping panty hose, a mirror, and tennis shoes in the car can enhance your image, increase your flexibility, and improve your efficiency.

The Traditional Homemaker originated this idea. In most cases, she needs to expand her supplies.

The Transitional Woman thinks it's a good idea, but she has doubts. She thinks the lip balm will spoil in the car, or the baby's toys will get dirty in the trunk, or the color of the wrapping paper will be wrong.

The Achieving Woman needs to expand her mini–office-kitchen and remember to use it.

**Bedtime Show-and-Tell**   Let the children know that your late night at the office or the time you spend with a friend is the same night as bedtime show-and-tell. That is, after you get home, you spend a little extra time with each child at bedtime. You read a story, let the child read to you, or simply talk about the day's events. The catch is that the children must be washed up, in their pajamas, and in their rooms by the time you come home. It is a pleasure coming home to children who are all ready for bed when you are late and tired. To allow the children time for bedtime preparations, you may have to plan a simple dinner for them. A breakfast dinner—that is, a dinner that consists of typical breakfast fare, such as bacon and eggs—is quick, nutritious, and can be made by husband or children. Or bring in pizza on show-and-tell night, or make arrangements with a babysitter to come every Tuesday night. Another option is to ask a neighbor or a SWAT team member to have your children over for dinner one night a week. You can spend that time with your sweetheart!

The Traditional Homemaker sometimes finds that declaring bedtime show-and-tell is the only way she can get her few hours a week of personal time.

The Transitional Woman thinks bedtime show-and-tell is a good idea, but she hates to impose on the neighbors or she feels that her children are burnt out on babysitters.

The Achieving Woman feels this tip offers a great way to enjoy both her professional life and her family life.

## Tips for Expanding Personal Time

Working women often overcommit to work and home activities and neglect personal time. Psychologists tell us that, to stay mentally healthy and happy, everyone needs personal time—time for themselves.

**The "Mom Is Off-Duty" Solution**  The working mom or woman simply lets the kids, herself, and her husband know that the time for "Mom, I need . . . "; "Janet, you must . . . ";

and "Honey, where is . . ." is over. Mom is going off-duty to read or do anything else she wants. Some women just disappear into a den or bedroom—children and husbands enter at their own risk.

The Traditional Homemaker welcomes this off-duty period, since she recognizes that she is on call most of the time.

The Transitional Woman would like to use this tip, but she feels guilty if someone really needs to say something to her and she is not "there" for them.

The Achieving Woman often uses this off-duty approach with her children, but she forgets how useful it is to have time away from other adults.

**The "Erase the Chalkboard" Approach**   Take one day a month to regroup, take a look at priorities, or do nothing but things you enjoy. Look at this day as "preventive sick leave." You will benefit because you are erasing nonessentials from your mental chalkboard and making room for essential mental notes. Your boss will benefit, because you come to work refreshed rather than working on overload, which is counterproductive. Your family will benefit because of your positive attitude.

The Traditional Homemaker has a hard time justifying this time away. Once she tries it, however, the benefits overshadow any negatives.

The Transitional Woman has a difficult time justifying sick leave if she is not ill and especially if she is not paid for this time off.

The Achieving Woman likes the idea but keeps putting it off. She is constantly on "fast forward."

When considering your time and tips for improving your use of it, focus on your lifestyle motivation and be careful to match your needs with your interests. It does work—give it a try!

## IMPORTANT POINTS TO REMEMBER

Your time is divided into professional, personal, and home components. Depending on your Personal Motivational Lifestyle, the amount of time you devote to each determines the amount of happiness, frustration, guilt, or anxiety you feel.

The Traditional Homemaker feels in control when the major time emphasis is on the home. The Transitional Woman feels she has more control over her life when the major time emphasis is equally divided between work and home. The Achieving Woman feels in control when the major time emphasis is on her career.

Time tips to expand professional time include development of the SWAT team and use of the all-inclusive month-at-a-glance calendar. Tips for home time are development of the mini–office-kitchen and bedtime show-and-tell. Strategies for expanding personal time include declaring mom off-duty and taking a day off to erase the mental chalkboard.

# 3

# AVOIDING THE GUILT TRAP: SELF-INDULGENCE IS A NECESSITY

Modern women find themselves trying to play demanding multiple roles. One woman may find herself meeting the responsibilities of a wife, mother, lover, and career woman—not to mention those of a friend, daughter, hostess, child schlepper, housekeeper, nurse, cook, and amateur shrink. Having to divide her attention between so many roles makes her feel guilty, so she redoubles her efforts by trying to excel in every one. No one can live happily or healthily under such stress, which can only lead to exhaustion. To break the cycle of guilt, stress, and exhaustion, self-indulgent activities are essential. They help the working woman balance all her roles.

## BALANCING TIME RATHER THAN JUGGLING IT

Most working women try to juggle their time between work, home, and personal activities. Just as in a juggling act, if one item is off balance, then the entire group is in

danger. It is one thing to plan your time, but another thing
to juggle it. Working women need to learn how to balance
time, not juggle it. Juggling requires perfect timing but
not flexibility. Balancing requires timing and a great
deal of flexibility.

Sally, an attorney who is married and has two small
children, shares how she turns time juggling into time
balancing. First, she refuses to work on weekends and does
little travel, unless it's a must. "I hire a babysitter to come
along on my out-of-town cases, which I keep to a very few.
My children have a good understanding of what I do and
how important my work is to me. They also know that my
love for them is even more important. My favorite holiday is Valentine's . . . I have this 'thing' for Valentine's. I
wonder how many male attorneys go home at the end of
working an eight- to ten-hour day and bake valentine
cookies?" Sally keeps her plans flexible on her out-of-town
trips. She knows flexibility is a must as a working mom.

Tammy and her husband have four children and own
their own business. Every school day, from 9:00 to 10:30
A.M., Tammy spends about 20 minutes in each of four
classrooms, to help out with her children. Tammy is there
to make sure they obtain a good education. "All they want
is attention—they don't want a tutor or a private school.
They want a mommy and daddy involved. I am not only
tutoring, but giving love."

Including the time she spends traveling to and from
the school, Tammy spends almost eight hours a week in
her active involvement with her children's education. Most
working parents can't take the time off their jobs to be
with their children during the day. "When I leave the office," says Tammy, "half the work force is gone." Asked how
she is able to accomplish this task, she says: "I made it an
obligation, like work. Their grades have gone up and up,
and it's changed their attitudes."

How can working women define their priorities and
act in accord with them even though major obstacles exist?

To help women do this, I have used four major reference points as tools.

## Define Your Priorities

In my time-management workshops, I ask women to use their imaginations to determine

- Characteristics they would like to develop
- How they really want to spend their time and with whom—not the way they would spend it to avoid guilt
- What they would do if money were not an issue
- How they would like to be remembered

The information gained from each of these determinations provides an important reference point in the landscape of time management. With reference points to outline priorities, time-management decisions become less difficult.

This section will present the questions used to determine each reference point. Use your imagination to answer each one, and see what priorities take shape.

**REFERENCE POINT 1: WHO OR WHAT WOULD YOU BE?**

If you could be anyone or anything in the world, who or what would that be? Once you have decided, write down as many phrases as you can that describe your choice. By studying your descriptions, you will probably get an idea of why your choice appeals to you. A good friend of mine would like to be a computer.

| | |
|---|---|
| *Who/What Would You Be?* | An IBM Computer |
| *Describe:* | It's small, streamlined, and fits comfortably on my desk. |

It's fast, powerful, and full of information.

It's not sensitive to others' emotions, only statements and directions.

Another friend of mine, a masseuse, would love to be Elizabeth Taylor.

| *Who/What Would You Be?* | Elizabeth Taylor |
|---|---|
| *Describe:* | She has seen and experienced personal and financial success. |
| | She has seen and experienced personal and financial failure. |
| | She has relearned many things and persisted. |
| | She is sexy and classic. |

By establishing reference point 1, working women can learn what characteristics they like, admire, and want to develop in themselves. This reference point gives the working woman "time direction," an idea of how she wants to develop and spend her work, home, and personal time.

What qualities do most women list as characteristics they aspire to have? When asked to list their responses under the heading "The Way I'd Like to Be," the top five characteristics for women under age 50 were:

- High earning
- Athletic
- Well educated
- Beautiful
- Patient

### REFERENCE POINT 2: WHAT IF YOU WERE MOVING?

What would you want to do or accomplish if you had only three months before moving to another state? With whom would you want to spend your time?

This reference point not only helps you clarify what you want to accomplish, but it helps you maintain a sense of perspective on those days when you can't seem to get anything worthwhile done. Janet, a marketing director for a small manufacturing business, recently had to take time from work to take her eleven-year-old son to the doctor— the child had a severe case of the flu. She spent 1½ hours waiting to see the doctor. Several weeks later, Janet took more time from work, because she wanted to see her son perform in a class play. "I rushed back to the office frazzled and had little time left to get work done. I just remember thinking, If this was my last day to live, did I waste my time this afternoon? Somehow, I calmed down and had to admit to myself that I was glad that I had taken the time to take my child to the doctor and to see his performance. It made me realize that even though I enjoy my job, my children make life worthwhile. The most important thing in my life is being with my family and sharing their experiences. That realization helps me keep my hectic life in perspective."

Working through reference point 2 helps working women realize how they want to spend their home and personal time—not out of guilt, but as a reflection of their priorities. The Traditional Homemaker, the Transitional Woman, and the Achieving Woman feel the same way: The quality of relationships is important. All three want to spend more time with their families and increase their personal time.

The Traditional Homemaker is more aware of her priorities than the other types. The Transitional Woman and the Achieving Woman are usually too busy doing to be aware.

Nancy decided to stay home with her four children while they were young. "I want to go to work after my children are in school. I don't want to miss them grow up. I can't believe my oldest is almost 12 years old. Another two years and the baby will be in school. I'm sure it'll whiz by."

**REFERENCE POINT 3: WHAT IF YOU WON THE LOTTERY?**

Working women have a tendency to think that if they did not have to earn money, they would not work. This may be true. But what would you do if money was not the reason for working? What if you won the lottery and became financially independent? Make a list of things you would like to do, accomplish, and spend your time on if money were not an issue.

The Traditional Homemaker will probably wish to remain unemployed but take more vacations with her significant others and purchase more or newer material possessions. She probably will wish for more time to do the things she and they enjoy. The Transitional Woman will find that half of her peers would stay home; the other half would continue working, but at a career where they felt more appreciated. She, like the Traditional Homemaker, would take more vacations and buy more material possessions. She would place greater emphasis on enjoying what she was doing. The Achieving Woman may find that she would keep most things just as they are and wish for more time to do everything else.

What does this mean to the working woman? In most cases it is *not* the money that determines who you want to be and what you want out of life; rather, these things are determined by *how much time you have*. Rather than feeling guilty for working or not working outside the home, it is healthier and more accurate to perceive money as a commodity and time as an asset.

Psychologists tell us that work creates purpose and worth in our lives but inactivity creates restlessness, boredom, and sometimes depression. Though most of us would want to change our way of life if we won the lottery, this reference point allows us to understand the need for activity and focus on those activities that are most meaningful.

Sandy, an Achieving Woman, says: "If I won the lottery, I'd invest 90%, pay off the house mortgage, and buy things for the family with the rest. I'd keep on working, but I would take one day a week and do anything I want or need to do. I'd go window-shopping, condition my split ends with mayonnaise, spend a day at the beauty shop, or stay home and finish projects—but I'd definitely keep working."

### REFERENCE POINT 4: WRITE A SPEECH IN YOUR HONOR

How would you like others to remember you? Imagine what you would like your parents, children, lovers, friends, and co-workers to say if they were asked to make a speech about you. What would you say if asked to describe your own accomplishments? This reference point helps put your values in order, just in case the other three have not yet done so.

When it's all said and done, how you want others to think of you now helps define who you really want to be. Knowing this will encourage you to spend time with those who are important to you. It adds to your enjoyment of life and increases your people-orientation—ultimately, the only activity that matters.

Susan, an accountant for a high school, oversees and is responsible for millions of dollars. She is newly remarried and has two sons in grammar school. She wakes up at 4:30 or 5:00 A.M. and is at work by 5:45. Susan's husband gets the children to Susan's office by 7:00. At 7:30, the school bus picks the children up at her office and takes them to school.

Susan's ten-year-old son makes TV commercials. At first, that seemed glamourous. But the glamour soon gave

way to the reality of the commute. Since Susan lives in
a small town, she must make a long drive to Los Angeles
for auditions. She usually has less than a 24-hour notice
for each trip. "I don't think I'll have enough money for
the boys to attend college if I don't do this now. When you
*do* get commercial assignments, the pay is great. A few years
of this, and I won't have to worry about their college
education.

"Our commute days are long. It's all worth it when one
of the children says, 'Thank you, mom, I appreciate all
you do for me.' This is the best speech in my honor that
the children could say. That's a great way to be thought of."

## REDUCING THE HIGH PRICE OF STRESS

Doctors tell us that anxiety, which produces stress, plays
a major role in illness. Stress is a factor in causing cancer,
migraine headaches, asthma, arthritis, and high blood
pressure—for starters. In addition, stress wastes a tre-
mendous amount of time. As an example, you need only
remember the last time you had a tension headache. Remember how it kept you from thinking creatively or
clearly, making decisions, finishing the task at hand, and
handling critical or sensitive situations? And don't forget the high monetary cost of anxiety. Medications and
doctors cost money, and employee illness is a major expense for employers.

Lynette, a secretary and a Transitional Woman, says:
"The doctor prescribed pills to settle my nerves, but it
made me more nervous. I spent over $50 a month on 'anti-
stress' pills. The medicine I took to relieve my tension only
made it worse. . . . I felt listless, depressed, and irritable
most of the time. A friend of mine talked me into going
to the gym. . . . Now I'm an exercise junkie. I don't feel one
ounce of guilt spending time at the gym, because now I

spend more time feeling well and enjoying the people in my life. I now feel more control over my life."

Therapists tell us that we can alleviate stress through exercising, eating healthfully, and pampering ourselves. When women under age 50 were asked, What would you do if you had an extra hour in the day?, the response was unanimous: "I'd spend it on myself." Only through effective time management can you achieve the freedom to give yourself the nurturing you want and that experts say is so necessary for you.

When viewed in comparison to the cost of the problems it can preclude, "self-indulgent" behavior might be the best bargain in town. The cost of a stress-reducing manicure or massage can seem low indeed in relation to the problems stress can cause. Consider the costs—both financial and psychological—of these common stress-related occurrences:

- Accidents
- Illnesses
- Forgetfulness
- Distraction

To beat stress, Michelle, an advertising representative, treats herself to monthly facials. "I feel that I have a lot more to give other people in my life if I pay attention to what is important to me and my own needs. That's why I don't feel any guilt taking time out for 'me.' I'm able to handle all the other stuff more easily if I've nurtured myself."

Ruth, a men's clothing buyer, says "I treat myself to weekly manicures, monthly facials, and monthly massages. If I had the money, I would have weekly everything, except swimming, for which I don't find the time. Nothing seems to calm me down more than my facials and massages. My chiropractor suggested the massages that I used to think were self-indulgent. Now, I look at them as

preventive medicine. I used to feel guilty taking the time
for me instead of finishing a project or spending the time
with my boyfriend. I don't know about other women, but
I find the time I spend on me helps me regenerate and
gives me a positive frame of mind."

## Examine Prevention Costs Versus Fix-It Costs: Case Studies

The difference between the cost of *preventing* a problem
and the cost of *fixing it* once it occurs is not mathematic,
but geometric. Let's look at some case studies that compare these costs. I think you will agree that guilt, anxiety,
and stress are extremely costly.

**The Situation**   On one hand, you're under a lot of time-
stress to complete a project at work; on the other, you feel
an obligation to help your child with homework. At work,
no one else has the information needed for completion;
at home, your eight-year-old is bringing in C's and D's in
math, your strong point.

**The Prevention**   *(a)* Ask for a one-day extension on the
project at work. In most cases, extensions are granted
without any ill effects. However, missing a deadline has
many ill effects. *(b)* Hire a tutor, be it a friend, an older
child skilled in math, or a professional suggested by the
school or teacher.

**The Cost**   *(a)* A little ego. *(b)* Dinner out or a dinner
made at home for the friend; a small thank-you gift or,
for $1.50, a thank-you card for the friend or child; $25 an
hour for the tutor.

**The Fix**   *(a)* Make excuses about why the project is not
complete, or "complete" it haphazardly. *(b)* Tutor your
child without a trace of patience, because you're thinking about the work that needs to be done at your office.

**The Cost** *(a)* Damage to your professional reputation, an increased level of guilt and stress that will stay with you for some time, and, possibly, accumulated stress that pours over into all relationships at work and at home. This cost is prohibitive! *(b)* An increased level of guilt and stress in your relationship with your child. This cost is also prohibitive!

**The Situation** You've been working hard at the office, your mom needs more attention because of a recent hospital stay, and your best friend is going through a divorce.

**The Prevention** Take some personal time off and go window-shopping, take an aromatic bath, go for a brisk walk or run, or do anything else that will help you get your mind off everything but something you find pleasurable. After you've spent some time nurturing yourself, call, rather than visit, your mom and friend. Be prepared to let them talk while you show your support by listening.

| **The Cost** | Window-shopping | $0.00 |
|---|---|---|
| | Scented bath | 0.40 |
| | Brisk walk or run | 0.00 |

**The Fix** You keep at your daily routine until you're so tired that you call in sick because your immune system is depleted.

**The Cost** Divide your monthly salary by 31, the approximate number of days in the month. This will give you your daily salary, more or less. Multiply the quotient by the number of days you are off work. Even if you have sick leave available and you are paid for this time-out, still figure the same cost.

Oh, by the way: If you missed one day, you now have eight hours less to complete your work. Remember that each sick day means one less work day.

## GUARDING YOUR OWN TIME

You've heard the saying "Do that on your own time, not my time." It describes a reality that we all face: the need to focus attention.

Sometimes it is your pleasure to pay attention to someone else. Sometimes it is your duty. Other times, however, it is your right not to pay attention to another person—to concentrate instead on something that you need to accomplish or that is fulfilling to you.

Each woman must set aside time for herself, which we'll call "my time." We'll call time that can be shared with someone else "your time." Guarding "my time" can be very difficult. You know how demanding a child can be when he or she wants attention when you are reading the newspaper—a valid use for "my time."

What's the solution? First, let other people know that the time you have set aside as "my time" is very special time for you and that you would appreciate not being interrupted during a specific period. In most cases, your statement will be all it takes.

When another person violates "my time," begin by using a liberal dose of patience. If the other person continues to take advantage of "my time," state assertively that even though you can appreciate occasional interruptions, he or she has gone too far.

In some cases, it takes serious repetition to get through to others. Molly, secretary and author, had to repeatedly tell her children she did not want to be disturbed or interrupted from 1:30 to 5:30 P.M. on Saturdays. When she remarried, she told her new husband, "You need to plan something for the children on Saturday afternoons. . . . I won't be available."

I asked Molly if her plan worked. "It took about a month before they really knew I was serious. My husband went off to do an errand and left the children at home while I was writing in my bedroom. One of my children knocked on the door. I said my normal, 'No, it's not 5:30 yet.' Again, a knock on the bedroom door; my daughter needed me right now. Again, I said, 'No, it's not 5:30 yet.' When my husband returned from his errand, he yelled into my bedroom that Jenny had fallen from the swing and had turned an ankle.

"We all immediately went to the hospital with Jen. She was on crutches for two months."

Because we are so used to thinking that responding to others' needs is part of a woman's role, setting limits on interruptions can be difficult for everyone at first. But, as in everything, assert your rights but stay flexible. Remind yourself that you have a right to time alone, but be aware that special circumstances do occur. Once family members are secure in the knowledge that you will be there in a real emergency, they might feel secure enough to let you alone for a while.

---

## IMPORTANT POINTS TO REMEMBER

Learn to balance, not juggle, your time. This will help you avoid the guilt trap. To help direct your priorities, keep four major questions in mind: What type of person do you want to be, what do you want to do or accomplish and with whom do you want to do it, what would you do if money were not an issue, and how do you want others to remember you?

Be aware of these questions during the times you feel guilty. I am confident they will not only direct you to constructive action, but help you make the transition from being guilt-ridden to being guilt-free.

# 4

# THE BIG GLITCH (WHEN THE BEST-LAID PLANS...)

---

Your day's mapped out—from jogging at 6 A.M., getting the children's breakfast and sending them off to school, to a breakfast meeting at 8 and appointments right on through a staff dinner meeting at the new hotel downtown. A jam-packed day, but you've scheduled your time realistically and have prepared in advance to avoid all possible glitches.

The jogging goes well, and your endorphins give you a lift that should carry you through the day. Then, just as you're turning into your driveway, your foot hits the sprinkler. You limp inside with a twisted ankle. Nothing serious—not enough to warrant a good war story, but enough discomfort to slow you down. Just as you're slipping into an Ace bandage (no time for ice), the phone rings. It's a colleague saying that she won't have her report finished in time for the staff meeting. Well, okay, you can handle it, but wait—from the den comes a piercing wail. You run to the rescue to find that Jimmy has dropped your 10-pound dumbbell on his foot. Now you're in real trouble, and it begins to look like a day that only Wonder Woman could salvage.

If you have no backup plans for such top-of-the-line catastrophes, you do all that any mere mortal can do. You carry your screaming child to the car; rush him and his broken toe to the emergency room; and, as soon as you can get to the phone, you ring your client. When he doesn't answer, you call the restaurant where your breakfast is scheduled and beg the hostess to explain your situation when the client arrives. A few minutes later, you dial your office, tell them what's happened, then hurry back to hold Jimmy's hand. In between these frantic moments, you try to put on a touch of makeup. You run a comb through your tousled hair and wonder if you can find someone to care for your traumatized tot later in the day.

## THE SWAT TEAM CONCEPT

Fortunately, this scenario need not occur. All you need to eliminate the problems and make things run smoothly is a SWAT team. What is a SWAT team? It's your personal group of special backup people who fill in at home or at work when you have a real emergency. I have many examples in my files of how successful SWAT teams have worked.

A friend of mine has one close neighbor as well as a nearby relative whom she calls her SWAT team. She has an agreement to call on them in genuine emergencies only. "I do *not* impose on these people for regular child-care needs or for trivial favors," she tells me. "But it's understood that, in times of crisis, they'll come running." The neighbor, who has a need for extra cash, is well paid for her work; the relative is rewarded with special tickets to art and theater openings.

Another working woman hires a retired nurse on a standby basis. For a small fee, the nurse agrees to take care of problems as they come up. "Many times," she explains, "this lady has been a savior. I can't tell you how much lost time she has saved me."

I talked about coping with the inevitable crisis with Terry Mayo, Los Angeles's first television anchorwoman. At the time, Terry was a divorced mother with a young son.

"I've always been a very positive person and believe strongly in the power of an optimistic attitude," she told me. "But as a parent, newswoman, business owner, and just plain fallible human being, I've gained a healthy respect for Murphy's Law."

Terry believes that life is unpredictable, especially life with children.

"Several months ago," Terry said, "I had scheduled a really important interview. Just as I was about to leave, my son, Chris, locked himself in the bathroom, the dog got loose, and someone drove by and swiped the side of my car . . . all within 15 minutes."

Luckily, Terry had an ace in the hole. She and Chris lived with her grandmother. Her live-in SWAT team took over almost instantly and allowed Terry to make her interview and deadline.

"I really believe in the idea of extended families," she said, "especially for single parents. I realize not everyone has a grandmother like mine, but single working mothers should really consider joining forces with an older woman, maybe someone who's widowed and lonely and needs to be needed as much as you need a warm, loving person to be there for your kids when you are away."

## HOW TO HANDLE UNEXPECTED ABSENCES FROM WORK

A SWAT team on the home front can go far in keeping the unscheduled time you take off from work to a minimum. The day will come, however, when some event in your personal life keeps you from making it to your job when the people at work are counting on you. Why not extend the SWAT team concept to your professional life?

## *Arrange for a Stand-In*

Sandy, a secretary for a medium-sized firm, had a home emergency the day her boss intended to present the annual report. Sandy had no choice but to call in and say "Sorry, I can't be there." Fortunately, however, she had a plan in place for just this sort of occasion. What Sandy did was to call in a trusted substitute, someone she knew who could handle the details. "Everything went wonderfully well," she beamed. "And at the end of the day, I sent my boss a bottle of wine with a personal note. Even now, a year later, he's still talking about what I did."

In another case, a schoolteacher I know well had to have an operation that would keep her off her feet for six weeks. "Long before I had to go in," she said, "I arranged with the school district for a trusted friend with a teaching credential to fill in for me."

During the time she was recuperating, her substitute kept her up-to-date with what was going on. As the teacher began to recover, she helped correct papers and offered advice about problems that occurred in the classroom.

## *Develop Personal Relationships*

Arranging in advance for a substitute is fine when someone else can do your job. But what about those meetings where you simply can't send a stand-in? What about lunch with your star client, for example? Such situations are tough. In the case of restaurant meetings, it pays to develop a relationship with the management and staff at one or two particular places.

Instead of table-hopping from one trendy bistro to another, I have developed relationships with the owners and staffs of one family-owned spot and one hotel restaurant. I get more than red-carpet service. In one instance, when I was forced to be an hour late for a meeting with a client, I called the owner-hostess, whom I know well, and asked her to seat my client, extend my apologies, and start him off with a glass of vintage wine and a special appetizer. When I arrived breathlessly, nearly 60 minutes later, I found him in a corner booth being happily pampered by my friend, Marie. As you might imagine, our meeting, though off to an unavoidable late start, ended on a high note.

## Go the Extra Mile to Apologize

Going the extra distance to make people happy after you've inconvenienced them is usually well worth the effort. Instead of an apologetic "I'm so sorry, but my sick child . . . " or "The tie-up on the freeway . . . ," recompense the other party.

A client of mine, an attorney, had to leave a client high and dry when she received a telephone call that her daughter was about to have an emergency appendectomy. "Of course," she told me, "he understood the problem. But after I returned home, I sent my client theater tickets with a personal note of apology."

Does this approach take too much time and expense? Not if you value your job and the people you work with. Let people know in a tangible way that you've reflected on the inconvenience you caused. If you do, you will stand out from the crowd. Jane, the attorney, was recently made a partner in her firm, and Sandy just received a major promotion. Don't expect others to suffer because you do. Being considerate of others, even in the midst of your own crises, will make them see you as someone truly special and not easily replaced.

## How to Set Up Your Own Swat Team

Once panic hits, it's too late to start crying "Help!" Most of us wouldn't dream of going through life without medical and car insurance; likewise, for anyone serious about her career (not to mention her family), playing ostrich and assuming that you'll "handle whatever happens when the time comes" is both arrogant and foolish. (Take it from someone who was foolish and lost a large contract because of it.)

There are any number of possible arrangements you can make when lining up emergency help. The key, of course, is to have at least two reliable people on call before you ever need them. Only call them during a real crisis; have other arrangements for your regular child-care needs. But, it's understood that, in times of a real crisis, they will be available.

Here's how to set up your team:

1. **Dream and list:** Identify people you know and respect. Think of friends who have children the same age as yours, neighbors whom you trust with children, or co-workers who might be free to take on extra tasks during evenings or weekends. Perhaps you know a new mother who isn't ready to go back to work full-time but who would welcome earning some occasional extra dollars. Or someone who's retired or between jobs. Check with local child-care directories, and always ask a child-care provider for references. Besides hiring outsiders, a number of women, like Terry Mayo, share a home with a relative or close friend. Could you ask the friend to help if there were a crisis? Others have had good luck with au pair girls— young women from other countries who come to the States on nine-month work visas. If you have a friend who uses an au pair, would your friend let you share the au pair in an emergency? (Hiring an au pair is often an excellent way to provide full-time child care; you may want to consider it.)

2. **Define:** Make sure team members agree on what is a true emergency. This will be covered in greater detail later in this chapter.

3. **Divide:** Take all the team members' names and organize them into categories. For example, know who you can call during a daytime crisis, a nighttime emergency, a weekend, when you're on an out-of-town trip, or when you're working late at the office.

An important digression: Only use your SWAT team when you need to and for the purpose it was intended. One abusive act will alienate that particular team member forever. Let the members of your SWAT team know, in advance, what category they fall under. And *always* thank them for their help by giving a card, flowers, movie tickets, singing telegram, balloons, a plant, dinner, or anything your budget will allow.

Don't be embarrassed to recruit team members. Chances are, you may be able to help each of them as much as they can help you. Go for it!

## WHAT CONSTITUTES A "REAL" EMERGENCY?

From my own archives and those of a number of close friends and clients, here is a list of the ten most common day wreckers:

- The totally sleepless night
- A leak, freeze, or other disaster in the home
- A medical emergency
- A summons to court
- The need to recover after being victimized
- The need to pay bills *fast*
- The need to move
- The big deadline

- The injury, illness, or death of a loved one
- The forgotten meeting

The sections that follow will discuss each of these un-welcome situations.

**The Totally Sleepless Night**   It doesn't matter why. Maybe Jimmy was up all night with the stomach flu, or perhaps you just ended a fling with the love of your life. In any case, a night without sleep ensures a hellish next day. If you don't feel you can call in sick (even though you may feel unprecedentedly wretched), try to give yourself a break. If at all possible, take a long lunch hour, then order something to take out and eat someplace where you can catch a snooze. Tell your co-workers that you're under the weather, and see if they can lighten your load. Maybe they'll let you slip away early—after all, you'd do, or have done, the same for them. When you can, go home, order a pizza, unplug the phone, and sleep.

**"Ma, Janie's Swimming in the Basement!"**   When the roof falls in at home and you can't wait until Saturday to have it repaired, try to pull off a miracle and get the repairer to come at a specified hour. (I know, it's equivalent to a parting of the Red Sea.) Otherwise, call in your SWAT team troops or, if you haven't done your homework, prevail on a neighbor to let in the repairer.

**When the Pain in Your Side Is Appendicitis**   If you find yourself facing emergency surgery, try to keep a cool head. (I didn't say this would be easy.) Call at least one reliable person to be your advocate while you're out of commission. Assume that you'll be a total basket case, and let him or her keep your affairs in order until you're well enough to shout orders from your bed.

**A Day in Court**   You were a good citizen and came forth with an unusually coherent account of an accident or crime. Now you're being rewarded by having to make an appearance in court, and you're missing valuable time at work. Make sure that all those who are losing your services are well acquainted with the reason for your absence. If possible, substantiate your explanation with a news clipping. If your absence is going to be extended, prepare for the worst (a deadlocked jury); get people to cover for you on all fronts.

**You, the Victim**   Your car has been totaled by a hit-and-run driver, or you come home from the movies and find that a thief has made off with everything from your stereo to your best lingerie. Besides the trauma of loss and invasion, you'll have to fill out police reports, insurance forms, and make arrangements for a new car (or negligee). All that is a day's work at least, so call in a substitute and then console yourself with the fact that your misadventure will make a great story.

**You, the Culprit**   You're a wizard on the job, not to mention a terrific human being. But somehow you neglected to pay those traffic tickets or utility bills, and you find yourself having to pay them in person—and immediately. (It's happened to some pretty prominent people.)

**Moving Day**   Moving is not exactly a full-fledged emergency; it is more of an expected crisis. Moving, even when it's from the slums to a penthouse, is a traumatic experience, and you can usually bet your paycheck that there will be a hitch or two. To minimize trauma, plan ahead. Try to move on a weekend. But if that's not possible, arrange to take a day or two off. The mistakes you'll prevent will save you time and money in the long run.

**The Big Crunch**   You've got a deadline and, in spite of heroic efforts, you're swamped. The best thing, of course, is to anticipate last-minute snafus and build up some "comp" time so you can finish that big report without having to pull an all-nighter or cancel important meetings. Should it come to that, call in your backups. Then bring roses to those who help you through. After all, *you* came out smelling like a rose!

**The Injury, Illness, or Death of a Loved One**   Do what you have to do and call in help from all sources. This is not the time to try to be the Rock of Gibraltar.

**A Meeting with Whom?**   You forget you scheduled a meeting with a client or someone at work. Do what you can to call in your SWAT team so you can make the appointment. If you are forced to cancel at the last minute or, worse yet, be a no-show, more than an apology is in order. Reschedule the appointment to suit the other person's convenience. Or reschedule the meeting at a restaurant, and you pick up the tab.

## IMPORTANT POINTS TO REMEMBER

Don't make the mistake of thinking that you'll be able to deal effectively with crises as they happen. Plan ahead by creating a SWAT team that can cover for you at home and at work. Make sure each SWAT team member knows exactly how you plan to use him or her, and don't abuse team members by calling on them for routine needs.

As you go along in your working life, you will find the SWAT team to be one of the finest tools in your arsenal. And, though you may not think so right now, you will find that—when used properly—you can use the team over and over again.

# 5

# *L'Affaire:* Making Time for Love (Married or Single)

Money, success, and power have their charms, but to most women a life without love is an incomplete one. Of all the kinds of love, Eros, or romantic love, provides an excitement unparalleled by other accomplishments. Love, like all things worth having, requires a time investment. Marriages and relationships that take a back seat to career, children, and social life tend to become stale and unrewarding.

## Planning for Romance

"I know that's what I want, and I know that's what I need, but where do I find the time for romance?" laments Georgia, an active entrepreneur. "I can't imagine having kids right now. I barely have time to be intimate with my fiancé. My business monopolizes every minute. It's amazing Steve still wants to marry me."

Most working women already have the skills they need

to find time for romance. When a working woman plans a meeting, she places the date and time on her calendar. When she has a project or a deadline, she takes the time and puts in the effort to finish on schedule. When she sets goals, she does what needs to be done to reach them. The same kind of planning and effort need to go into making time for romance. If work is important to you, you work. If an activity is important to you, you do it. If romance is important to you, you plan for it.

## Assess Your Current Number of Romantic Hours

As discussed in Chapter 2, chart the time you spend with your lover or thinking about your sensuality. Romantic time is personal time. Almost all working women need to increase the time they spend enjoying this activity.

## Increase Romantic Time

Most women say they would love to add three romantic, personal hours to their lives each week. Let's look at some ways to do this:

- Three times a week, go to bed an hour early. If your normal bedtime is 9:30 P.M., go to bed at 8:30 and spend that extra time talking to your lover in person or over the phone (talking is the first part in making love), reading a steamy novel to each other, or thinking about sexual fantasies.

- Each week, set up three one-hour sessions for romantic time. Allow no television, no meetings, and no work. Just as you plan to take lunch from noon to 1:00 P.M., you must plan for your romantic time. If weekday evenings are bad, try weekend evenings, afternoons, or mornings. Choose a time and see if it works. I have always believed in the cliché "Where there's a will, there's a way."

- Plan three meals with your lover weekly. Try a breakfast, lunch, and dinner, or try two lunches and
  one dinner. However, do your best to keep the
  same days and times so that you establish the habit
  of blocking out those times on your calendar. Re-
  fuse any other commitments at those times. Out
  of 21 meals a week, coming up with 3 should be
  easy.

- Ask permission to take 30 minutes extra time during one lunch hour each week. Make the time up
  if necessary. Your long lunch with your lover will
  be a wonderful entrée to private time.

- Treat your romantic self and your lover to 3 hours
  of time alone together. Your time could be Saturday or Sunday morning or during midafternoon,
  late afternoon, or evening. Plan for the children's
  care and pretend you're out of town—go sight-
  seeing or for a quiet walk. Such a get-together takes
  little money, and you're only gone for three hours
  rather than an entire weekend or day.

- Change your mind-set. It is important that you *believe*
  that your romantic self is as important as your professional or home self. I believe the romantic self
  is the most genuine and real of all roles.

- Agree to a planned "surprise" time once a week or
  once a month. During this time, one partner agrees
  to surprise the other by planning an event. The
  event could be as simple as an ice-cream cone and
  a walk around the park or as elaborate as a weekend
  trip. There are two purposes to surprise time: the
  first is that one person tries to please the other by
  planning an event that both will enjoy; the second
  is that the responsibility for pleasing alternates from
  person to person.

  You may also want to try springing unplanned surprise time on your partner. Without warning, try

"kidnapping" your husband or lover. The results can be very exciting and a great success.

- Establish holidays as romantic times. During holidays set aside a certain time when you and your lover can be alone. If you have children, arrange to have them taken care of for a few hours. This gives these days special meaning.

- Once in a while, when you're both up to your ears in work, set a time to get together for a drink, coffee, or lunch. The outing will act as an escape valve. Though finding the time may seem impossible, remember: You can usually find a way to do what you really want to.

## UNDERSTANDING YOURSELF

Bonnie, a psychologist, says that how a women sees herself is directly related to how she acts in a love relationship. "In other words, if a woman feels unattractive about her face or body, she often finds it difficult to become intimately close." As this example indicates, the first step to examining our own intimate relationships is to understand the mind-set we bring to them. Once again, the three types of women introduced earlier—the Traditional Homemaker, the Transitional Woman, and the Achieving Woman—offer insight into typical attitudes. See if you find your own viewpoints reflected in the next three sections.

### The Traditional Homemaker

Bonnie, the psychologist, describes a problem that's common among Traditional Homemakers: "Women who stay home become dependent on family and friends for outward compliments." Bonnie believes that "the stay-at-home women often feel that life is passing them by while their working friends have it all."

## The Transitional Woman

The Transitional Woman has a strong awareness of her life script. Sometimes, Bonnie says, she may get caught in it. "Suppose you think your life script says 'You must be a good daughter, wife, mother, or friend first. If you're going to work, it should rank behind all other responsibilities.' You will take the time to nurture everyone else but yourself. You're caught in a cultural value system that holds the belief that you work to help the family. When a woman like this finds her work rewarding, she feels guilty. This is especially true if she can now stop working for financial reasons. She feels ambivalent about letting her newfound freedom go. She feels 'whole.' But time-pressures get the best of her. She feels better as a person, but juggles her work and family life. She keeps hoping for the day when she can focus on her romantic self."

## The Achieving Woman

The Achieving Woman expects a lot from herself and from others, lovers not excluded. She is so busy doing that she often fails to recognize the need to love and be loved. Of the three types of women, the Achieving Woman is the most likely to be a workaholic. "Women who are workaholics prefer to work rather than do anything else," says Carol, a family therapist. "They have a tendency to go through cycles. They put a lot of effort into their work, and then they wear down or burn out, and repeat the cycle. They are susceptible to the need to nurture others during their downtime. However, they have a strong need to be nurtured themselves."

## GOING ON DATES

Earlier in this chapter, you read a list of suggestions for
finding three extra hours for romantic time each week.
One of the suggestions, setting up a regular time to be
alone with your partner—that is, making a date—is so important that it deserves a section of its own. If you can
set aside only one hour for each date, that's fine; if you
can set aside more time, even better.

Begin by looking at your calendars and deciding on
the time you both can set aside to be alone together. Are
Tuesday afternoons between 11:30 A.M. and 12:30 P.M.
good? Or would Wednesday evenings be better? If no time
seems ideal, choose two and toss a coin to determine your
date time. The two most important things to remember
are to *set* the time and to *KEEP* it! No excuses—except,
perhaps, hospitalization.

Jenny, a college instructor, sets aside Wednesday night
for her lover. "It could be raining, snowing, or anything
else, but we don't give up our night together. It's the only
time I really feel I have his undivided attention."

Marjorie says that being together for only a little while
"keeps my husband and me in touch with each other. I
know it doesn't seem like much, but it really helps. Once
in a while, we'll forgo dinner out and go to a hotel together. There's something exciting about that."

Sydney, a caterer, plans Thursday evenings for her date
night with her husband. She is totally committed to this
time and will not accept any catering jobs for these evenings. "David and I have been married 17 years. When I
started my catering business eight years ago, I promised
myself that I would not forget my husband. I know I have
lost a lot of business because of this Thursday-night date
night, but I also know that it proves to my husband how
important he is to me. *No* amount of money can buy that."

Sandy, like Sydney, has discovered the fulfillment of
her relationship with her husband. She has been an attor-

ney for over 15 years and was a pharmacist before that.
Sandy has four grown children and has been married for
25 years. "Everyone said that I would have to work late
nights and every weekend. Most of the attorneys in my office do just that. Usually I am home by 6:00 P.M., and I
rarely go to the office on weekends. I'm not mega-wealthy,
but I do OK. After all, how much can I eat, or how many
cars can I drive, or how large of a bed- and bathroom do
I need?

"I see a lot of my fellow attorneys divorce because they
let their careers take over their lives and values completely.
I see how miserable they are when they work all the time
and fail to make time for the people they love."

A date can consist of staying in or going out, of just
holding hands or of steaming up the windows. The next
sections will give you a few ideas for spending your special
times together.

## A Crockpot and Wine

Janey, a nutritionist, puts a lot of effort into making the
time with her husband. "It's not easy to make a relationship work. I'm the one who plans 'special time.' If it weren't
for the planning that I do, I think we would see each other
only when we pass in the bathroom."

Janey and her husband enjoy stay-at-home dates, for
which Janey goes to the trouble of making a home-cooked
meal—or as she puts it, "a crockpot-cooked meal." She
adds to the occasion by bringing home a bottle of wine.
They begin their special time together by enjoying dinner.

"During this time my husband puts all work away.
Some of our best talks occur on these evenings. We don't
answer the phone, the door, or anything else. We look forward to these times. And, once in a while, he takes over
and does the planning."

Not everyone can expect to find a time at home when
they can enjoy each other. This is especially true if you

have children. Many working women feel that their home is not a quiet haven until 10 P.M., and then they're usually too tired to do anything except sleep. These women and their lovers need to leave the house to really enjoy their date.

## An Hour or Two Out

Marjorie works at home, taking care of four children under the age of 12. Her days are filled with crying children, cleaning, cooking, diaper changing, and afternoon chauf-feuring. "When I feel particularly frazzled, my husband and I go out to dinner. I don't work, so we try to make ends meet on one salary. We don't go anywhere fancy, but it doesn't matter, because we are *out* of the house. Jim likes it too because it gives him some quiet time with me."

The feeling that "I don't bring in a paycheck, therefore, we can't spend too much money," is a common one among Traditional Homemakers. The stay-at-home woman has a difficult time realizing she has far fewer expenses than the woman who works outside the home. When mother stays home, there are fewer expenses for child care, con-venience foods, working clothes, and more.

Setting aside a regular time for a date is important, but never let the date become routine. Don't hesitate to go on a date at a time that's not your regular date time, and be creative about incorporating surprises and treats into the event. Sarah, a receptionist, and her husband decided to go on a special date for Valentine's Day, and her husband made it all the more special by planning a surprise for her. "For Valentine's Day this year my hus-band had to work, so we celebrated the next night. He got all dressed up, went outside, and rang the doorbell—my children thought he had flipped out. I answered the door, and we went out to dinner at our favorite little Japanese restaurant. He surprised me and made reservations at a hotel. He even brought the teddy he had given me the day before, [as well as] our toothbrushes, toothpaste, and other toiletries.

"We got to the room around 9:30 P.M., and he opened a bottle of champagne. It was the same champagne bottle we were going to drink on New Year's Eve, but we didn't because that turned out to be a disaster. Two of our three children were in a play that night, and one of the boys was just recovering from a bad case of the flu.

"Well, we stayed at the hotel until midnight, then went back home to spend the night with the children. When we got home at 12:30 A.M., my oldest complained he was congested and couldn't sleep. I gave him his medicine, turned on the humidifier, made some hot tea, and put a hot compress over his nose and sinuses.

"The next morning, my husband and I woke up at 9:00 A.M., left the children sleeping, and went back to the hotel room. We got home by 1:00 P.M. I felt as though we had had an entire weekend—and we were only gone for 9½ hours total!"

## Sexy Times

Kerri describes the situation that results when work and responsibilities crowd out sex: "My work and my children take so much of my time. Our sex life had become boring and harried, when we got around to it." Kerri and her boyfriend of six years solved the problem by setting aside a time each week to check in to a hotel. This secret getaway helped put spice back into their relationship. And the advantage of having no distractions in their hotel room created a sexy mood that made their time together more exciting.

Kerri and her boyfriend discovered that planning was the key to sex as well as romance. When working women focus their efforts on planning for romance and sex, the results are often as successful as when they focus their efforts on an office project. Both take planning, initiative, and follow-up for best results.

Psychologists tell us that men get sexually aroused by sight, and women get sexually aroused by "good" communication. It makes sense to combine sight with communication. The key is to *plan* on it.

Shawna is a cosmetologist who owns her own spa and salon. She and her husband spend Friday nights making psychologists all over the world happy. She gets to her salon early on Friday mornings so she can leave about two hours earlier than on other days. "I come home, unwind a little, spend some time with the children, take them to a friend's house, and come home and get ready for the evening."

Shawna gets ready by putting on something sexy. "My husband loves to see me in negligees and teddys. Actually, I feel sexy when I'm wearing one. We make dinner together and sit and talk. We have only one rule: No touching until after dinner. Somehow this increases the excitement and yet allows us to have nice, long conversations at the dinner table. Once in a while, we break the rule.

"We play a game. We make love in a different room each time. The first time we tried our bathroom; we roared the entire time. The other room we spend a lot of time laughing in is our laundry room. You'd be surprised at how large washers and dryers can be. This is not only sexy, but it's also a lot of laughs."

Susan, who takes care of three school-aged children, has a "late-night" husband. She adjusts to his schedule so that they have some quiet time together. "I learned a long time ago that if I wanted to spend quality time with my husband, I better learn to take little catnaps during the day. Not only can I now keep up with someone who stays awake until 1:30 A.M., I take some of that time to work on several hobbies that I enjoy. It's extra quiet very late at night."

## Five Topics Not to Discuss on a Date

It is vital, during a date, that you make five subject areas off-limits: finances, children, past flames (including ex's), bad decisions made in the past, and in-laws. These topics will undermine your date faster than anything else. They are emotionally fueled and anxiety driven.

I am not suggesting that you do not talk about these important issues. Just put them aside on dates. This time is just for you and your lover to share what you like about each other and your concerns, your feelings, and your love.

"After several sessions in therapy with my husband, I realized that I do still like him," says Melanie. "I knew I loved him deep down, but we always get into fights about finances. Now we discuss finances at our weekly problem-solving session. We laugh a lot more now."

Children are demanding. Disciplining children is emotionally draining, particularly as they get older. Even when two parents agree on child-rearing practices, it's difficult. When parents disagree, it's similar to an erupting volcano. "Jim and I are complete opposites when it comes to raising children," says Christie. "I am by far more strict. He just lets our teenagers get away with murder.... We've come to an agreement: I discipline during the week, and he does it on the weekends. It's not perfect, but we don't spend what little time we have together fighting over the kids."

Discussing ex-sweethearts is also hard on the emotions. "No matter how much Jerry tells me he loves me, when he mentions his ex, I get all bent out of shape. We can have a perfectly nice time together until he brings up his former girlfriend. Sometimes I think I'm the most jealous person in the world, but my friends feel the same way when it happens to them."

Most couples, if they spend any time together, do not always make the correct choices or decisions. One husband says: "Joan and I have a good relationship. I must admit though, I get angry when she brings up bad decisions I've made. We've kinda worked it out. She doesn't bring up the 'old wash,' and I don't talk about my ex."

In-law jokes are for television shows and cocktail parties. The tales of in-laws are not funny when a couple argues over them. Sandy says: "We decided a long time ago not to discuss anything negative the in-laws do. I used to get hurt when his mom would knock my cooking or housecleaning habits. Now we consciously make an effort to laugh at the in-laws' idiosyncracies."

## Making Time for the Romantic You

As working women, we know how important our personal time can be. Usually, by the time we do what we feel we have to do in the course of a day, it's time to go to bed or back to work. It is important to take your personal time and use it in any way that makes you feel happy, restful, or romantic. Making time for your romantic self is just as important as taking the time to do any other personal activity.

It is essential that working women *plan* for personal time. The Traditional Homemaker needs to know that she has earned quiet, personal time to be a woman and feel feminine, pretty, or just at peace with herself. Often, she will do everything in her power to nurture and make others feel good but cheat herself of special sensations. She feels that the description *romantic woman* does not include her.

The Transitional Woman needs to know that she also has earned personal time to be with herself and get to know herself better. These women are so busy just keeping up with everyday activities, they forget about their needs, particularly in sexual areas. Bonnie, the psychologist, says: "Women caught in the middle of wanting to stay home and wanting to go to work are hardest hit psychologically and emotionally. They literally have not made any time for themselves, romantically or otherwise."

The Achieving Woman needs to learn to slow down and keep herself on her priority list. These women focus most of their energy and momentum on their jobs and careers; they concentrate on how to do a task better, attract more clients, increase cash flow, reorganize a department, increase staff participation and output, or create a new project. They appreciate the feminine and sexy lingerie in magazines and catalogues but do not make the time to purchase these items for themselves.

Working women of all types must start a personal game plan that makes time for their romantic selves. Here are a few ideas that will help get you more in touch with your womanhood:

- Take long, luxurious baths.
- Visit stores and try on lingerie.
- Buy one sexy undergarment each month.
- Treat yourself to something that makes you feel special, pretty, or sexy.
- Rent that romantic movie you love to watch.
- Go somewhere dressy with your lover and tell him, halfway through the evening, that you're not wearing any underwear.
- Go somewhere dressy and show a little cleavage. All the models on magazine covers do it.
- Go shopping and try on sexy dresses.
- Curl up with a "sizzling" book and reread the sleazy scenes.
- Think about what you will do and what your lover will do to you tonight; get mentally prepared and the body follows.

- Listen to soft music and think about some fun times.
- Go see an X-rated movie.
- Call up a friend and go out for the evening.
- Sit around a fireplace listening to music, reading, or talking to a good friend.
- Make an appointment at the photographer's to have a "glamour" picture taken.
- Try a good cup of coffee and a good magazine.

Any one of these tips should help you regain contact with the real you, gain perspective on your life, and provide you with the psychological resources you need to live the life you want to live.

Sometimes making time for the romantic you can take some basic restructuring. But fundamental change is possible; Candace's story is a case in point. Candace, a single woman, used to stay at the office until 6 P.M. and then go home and fix herself a quick dinner of leftovers or cottage cheese and fruit. Then she'd start working again. She and her boyfriend spent little time together. One day, Candace realized that she didn't want to spend her life alone, without the pleasures and communication of love. She told her boss that her work load was too great for one person and that she had no life outside work. They discussed what they could do to assign Candace a reasonable work load. "I knew my boss appreciated my efforts and had confidence in my ability. I took a big risk though, because I did not have another job to fall back on if he said 'quits.' I was ready for the risk. I was to the point that I needed to make a positive change in my life. I gambled and I won. I am much happier now and feel my life is more balanced."

## IMPORTANT POINTS TO REMEMBER

Working women need to restructure their thinking. They need to think of themselves and their personal needs as much, if not more, than others' needs. As psychologists note, when the woman feels good about herself, her positive attitude touches others.

There is no mystery in finding time to be with your lover. Rather, it is a matter of blocking out time, scheduling, and planning for dates that help keep the love spark alive. Women who put as much energy into scheduling time for themselves as for their lovers are winners on both fronts.

Keep your get-togethers positive and loving. Nurture your relationships, including your relationship with the romantic you. Be good to yourself. You deserve it!

# 6

# CREATIVE EARNING OPTIONS

---

Part-time work used to be a way for women to pick up a few extra dollars. It included all manner of employment, from stuffing envelopes to minding the local boutique for a few hours. But with the current (and no doubt permanent) need for more money, part-time jobs that pay minimum wage seldom warrant the effort.

Today, a woman must be creative when she assesses her earning capacity. She must evaluate many employment options—job sharing, flextime, working at home, starting a franchise, and running her own business, to name a few—and determine which will give her the money she needs and the peace of mind she deserves. What's more, she may have to convince others that an alternate way of working is viable.

---

## DETERMINING YOUR NEED FOR AN ALTERNATE EMPLOYMENT STYLE

Many women must meet so many demands that, to preserve their family lives and sanities, they need a work schedule that is more flexible than traditional 9-to-5 employment. Working women need to understand that they will progress through different life stages. A working woman may feel compelled to job-share a position after her child is born or during a later stage in life, for example. Here's how to recognize if you are a prime candidate for a different employment style:

- You are mentally and physically exhausted every day.
- You come down with colds and other viruses often.
- You are irritable all the time.
- You look forward to Friday on Monday.
- You go to bed at midnight just to keep up with the housework and wash.

If you are one of these exhausted women, the number of alternate employment options will come as a comfort to you. The next section will discuss job-sharing, one of the most common alternate earning styles.

## EVALUATING JOB SHARING

About the only viable way to nail down bona fide career-caliber employment part-time is to join forces with someone with like abilities. Then sell yourself as a package deal. In other words, share a job.

Most jobs can be flexible enough to accommodate sharing. In *Workforce 2000: Work and Workers for the 21st Century*, William B. Johnston and H. Arnold Packer reveal "Part-time, flexible, and stay-at-home jobs will increase, and total work hours per employee are likely to drop in response to the needs of women to 'integrate work and child-rearing.'"

If one or more of the following statements apply to you, job sharing could be for you:

- You have a commitment to your job or career.
- You need to spend more time on personal issues and your family.

- You need time to regroup.
- After-school child care is not always available.
- You want or need to spend more time with young children.
- You want or need to work during a difficult pregnancy.

There are several types of job-sharing schedules that you can discuss with your employer. One of the following case studies may give you an idea of a schedule that could work for you.

Cindy, an attorney for the public defender's office, alternates between working two days a week and three days a week. Another female attorney is at Cindy's desk on business days when Cindy is not. The two women have been taking care of their caseload in this fashion for over 2½ years. "I didn't know if this was really going to work when we first started. Everyone looked at us as if we weren't *real* attorneys, but after we started winning a few cases, very few people gave us 'the look.' I don't think this could work if my partner and I didn't speak on the phone a dozen times a day. After all, you have someone's life at stake here."

Similarly, Heidi, a court reporter with two small children, and another court reporter take turns working. Heidi works one week, and the other court reporter works the next week. "This arrangement works," Heidi says, "because I finish my cases at home if I have to. My boss thought I was nuts when I first suggested this four years ago. There weren't a lot of court reporters available then, so I don't think he had much of a choice. But he's never regretted the decision."

## ASSESSING THE POTENTIAL FOR FLEXTIME

Susan, an accountant, gets to work at 7:00 A.M., takes a 30-minute lunch break, and leaves the office at 3:30—1½ hours before employees who work a traditional schedule. "I put in the same amount of hours as everyone else, and I'm home when the kids arrive. My boss has offered me a raise because he is pleased with my performance."

Susan's work schedule is a classic example of flextime, a system of working that allows an employee to choose, within limits, the hours spent at work.

Another common form of flextime allows employees to work fewer days a week. Municipal-court judges have developed a 4-10 program, which means the judges work four days a week for 10 hours a day. This program provides judges time to spend with their families or to pursue other activities.

As the next section will discuss, flextime offers advantages to employers as well as solving problems for employees. Nevertheless, those who propose flextime or other alternate work styles may have to do a lot of convincing to get others to go along.

## CONVINCING AN EMPLOYER

Studies show that job sharing, flextime, and other options that make an employee's time more flexible (these options will be discussed later in this chapter) benefit the employer. If you find yourself having to convince your employer to experiment with an alternate employment style, make sure you mention the points that follow.

Alternative employment:

- Increases productivity
- Increases loyalty
- Results in less absenteeism
- Is a business's social responsibility
- Allows, in the case of job sharing, the business to tap the creative juices of more than one mind

## FINDING OTHER WAYS TO LIGHTEN THE JOB LOAD

In addition to changing your work schedule, you may be able to improve the quality of your life by changing your vacation schedule and child-care arrangements.

### *Comp Days and Personal Days*

More time off can give you the breathing space you need to feel human again. Some employers are receptive to granting time off in lieu of overtime pay. Such time off is called compensatory time, or "comp" time.

Jenny found that comp time helped her remove much of the time-pressure that was stressing her. Jenny's job takes her traveling six weeks out of the year. With her employer she has worked out a plan that allows her to spend two comp days at home after a week-long trip. "These two extra days help me feel grounded again. The comp time helps me deal with jet lag, groceries, housework, and I'm able to play with my baby for two straight days. I usually check with the office when I'm on comp days. If I have to make return business calls, I do it from home. I love my job, but there's also a domestic side to me. These extra days make it work."

Sarah's job doesn't require travel, but she finds there are a lot of peaks and valleys in her activity level at her job. For instance, the company frequently has one or two rush jobs a month, and these jobs sometimes require 12-hour days for three or four days. Then everything returns to normal for a few days—until another rush order comes in. After a few months of this, Sarah approached her employer, explained the stress caused by this kind of schedule, and suggested she be allowed a comp day after one or two of these particularly busy periods. Her boss agreed. "Before," Sarah says, "I hated the extra work load. Now, since I know I'm going to get some extra time off, I really look forward to the extra work."

Increasing the number of personal days you are allotted can have the same effect as increasing the number of comp days.

I have worked with several companies over the years and suggested that they give one personal day per month to each employee. The departments that use this approach have had higher morale, 36% higher productivity, and far less employee absenteeism. The company that implements this plan both shows and tells its employees how important they are to the business, and shows how the company views personal and family needs. Jon, a systems analyst, says: "We have seen a complete turnaround in morale since we started this program three years ago. In fact, we're thinking of adding one more day each month. Our main competitor locally has just begun the 'personal day a month' program. They'll flip when they find out we've decided to give two days."

Some companies are reluctant to try this, since, on the surface, one day a month represents another two weeks of vacation per employee per year. To convince any company you work for that increasing the number of personal days makes sense, you will need to present a convincing argument. Try using the sort of argument that Janet, an insurance adjuster, used.

Janet had a particularly heavy work load. As a result, she found herself becoming tired and discouraged. What she needed, she decided, was some additional time off each month. After she made her request, her boss turned her down flat. Janet then began to keep records of the work she was expected to complete . . . and the amount she was actually able to finish on schedule. After a couple of months of this, she reapproached the boss. She asked him to try an experiment. Give me a personal day off for two months, she said, and then look at the output. If it didn't go up, she wouldn't ask again.

"Somehow," Janet said, "that extra day a month relaxed me. It also gave me a new perspective on work. I came back after that first 'vacation day' and increased my production by 6%. The second month, it was almost 15%. Armed with this, I convinced the company to not only give *me* this extra time, but all of the other adjusters as well. Now the company says it will never go back to the other system."

If you want extra vacation or personal days, approach the matter as Janet did. First, think about your job for a few days to see if you feel that an extra day off would increase your production. Keep records of what you are doing now, work up a convincing argument, and approach your boss with it. Don't ask for a permanent change; ask for a trial period. If he or she agrees, document what happens and make sure the boss knows the result. If the boss disagrees, rework your approach and try again in a few months.

If the company you work for can't give you one personal day per month with pay, ask for half a day per month or a half or full day every other month. See if you can create a reasonable plan that will enable you to come back to work refreshed and in a good frame of mind.

## Child Care

More and more, prospective employees ask their employers-to-be what type of child care they offer. When the competition for employees is stiff, the company that offers child care will be the one that wins the talent.

The Child Care Action Campaign, a New York City–based coalition of leaders in the child-care field, found that "of 5,000 workers with young children at five Midwestern corporations, 48 percent of the women and 25 percent of the men felt their worries about their children made their work time less productive."

According to John Fernandez, author of *Child Care and Corporate Productivity*, "Caring for a sick child led 82 per-cent of the women surveyed to miss work more than six times during the previous year. For men, the figure was 58 percent." It is estimated that businesses lose up to $3 billion each year due to child care–related absences.

## WORKING AT A HOME OFFICE

If your job does not require you to be at the office every day, you may want to negotiate an arrangement that lets you work one day a week at a home office. Naomi has a demanding job, and she had just given birth to her second baby. "When I had Chelsea (my second baby), working five days a week put an extra strain on me and my marriage. I love my job, and I know I'd be bored at home full-time. I asked my boss if I could work away from the office on Wednesdays. I don't get as much work done at home that I would at the office, but my spirits are better and I feel I have a better handle on my life."

Rebecca, who has fewer distractions at home than Naomi, found she could get more done by working out-side the office than in it. Four days out of five, Rebecca writes reports for her boss. This requires her complete concentration, but at the office her fellow employees kept coming in to consult with her; the boss herself kept inter-rupting. As a result, Rebecca had trouble getting anything done at the office. To solve this problem, Rebecca sug-gested that she spend at least one day a week working at home—preferably, two days. Reluctantly her boss agreed to try the idea for at least a week or two. "Since I wasn't constantly starting and stopping, my production jumped immediately," Rebecca said. "I finished a report that first day that would normally have taken three days at the office."

## Opening a Franchise

Franchising is an option that is helping many women build more flexibility into their schedules. Buying an existing franchise business or concept eliminates many of the problems of starting a business from scratch. Your service or product has a track record, and the franchisor can offer you operational techniques, advertising, marketing, and other excellent benefits. However, a stumbling block for many women is the initial franchise fee and start-up capital needed. In addition, the franchisee must pay royalties—a percentage of gross sales—to the franchisor on a regular basis.

Top money-earning franchises for women, according to *Entrepreneurial Woman* magazine, are A Choice Nanny, Auntie Anne's, The Coffee Beanery, Conroy's, Critter Care, Cruise Holidays, Decorating Den, HouseMaster of America, Jazzercise, and Jenny Craig. (See the July/August 1992 issue of *Entrepreneurial Woman* for other top franchises for women. The issue also lists the addresses and phone numbers of the franchisors.)

## Starting Your Own Business

There are more than seven million women-owned businesses in the United States. This number has doubled since the early '80s. In fact, since 1982, the Small Business Administration has recorded twice as many business startups for women than for men. The National Association of

Women Business Owners, the largest women business owners' association, estimates that 32% of its members have children at home. Working mothers with children under the age of 18 increased within the last year.

More and more women start their own businesses, and they do so for a myriad of reasons. Freedom and personal fulfillment are two of the primary reasons, according to a recent MasterCard Business Card Survey.

In addition, women want to be decision makers, have more flexible work schedules, change careers, and start something from scratch to see if their efforts can make it successful. Women have started businesses in every industry, from bookkeeping to high tech. Personally, I would like to see more working women do this.

The increase in outsourcing offers opportunities for women who own small businesses. For large businesses to downsize and stay profitable, they are contracting for work that was previously done in-house. IBM, for example, recently eliminated its real estate department and contracted with an outside real estate firm. Many businesses are outsourcing their data processing and bookkeeping departments. For the female entrepreneur who wants to start her own business, outsourcing is an important trend to note.

Let's look at several job categories and see the potential each offers to a woman with the qualifications, experience, and motivation.

**Accountant**   An accounting business can be started with little capital. An adding machine, pencils, and a word processor would make a good start. Small-business owners are usually in need of accounting services.

Vera was let go after her company started to downsize. "Everyone was sad to see me go, because they liked my work. I thought if my boss thought I was doing a good job, maybe he would be willing to hire me by the hour and not pay benefits and worker's compensation. It worked. I started with 10 hours a week, and now I have a part-time employee helping me out during tax season."

**Sales Representative**   Most businesses could use a good sales representative to show and sell services or products. Working strictly on commission, around your hours, is like having your own business.

**Public Relations Specialist**   You need a two-line phone system and a computer and printer to get started. Most business owners need effective public relations but are too busy to do it themselves.

Edith worked for a large firm as a public relations representative until her second child was born. "I didn't know if I was coming or going after Cindy's birth. I couldn't think of anything but diapers and rashes. I had to take off a lot of time because my newborn was allergic to almost everything. I decided to start a public relations firm on my own turf and on my own terms."

**Provider of Seminars and Training**   Suppose a woman has significant knowledge and expertise in a particular field. Why shouldn't she charge a fee to share what she knows? The fields of finance and management present many opportunities for a provider of seminars and training.

Donna sold her tow truck company after owning it for 15 years. She now gives seminars in a variety of subject areas: proper dress for business, telephone techniques, leadership development in middle management, and developing relationships with bankers. "A lot of these things I had to learn from the seat of my pants," she said.

**Editor**   A dictionary, red pencils, and experience in producing manuscripts for businesses or publishers would start this business. All types of publishers are overwhelmed with written material. You can edit this material to meet publisher's standards and needs. You can also help authors who don't have a clue as to how to handle their writing.

Diana was a senior editor at a large publishing house until she was laid off. "My former publishing company hired me piecemeal to read manuscripts. It took me two years of editing would-be writers before I was making my old salary. I didn't have much in the way of self-esteem for the first few years, but it all worked out . . . finally."

**Speech Therapist**   Start with the required certification and education and a telephone. Add a working knowledge of Spanish or some other language, and you are even more of a drawing card. Studies indicate that more and more children enter school with speech difficulties, so a business providing speech therapy could offer an enterprising woman a bright future.

**Secretary**   Good secretaries are priceless. With a second-hand computer, paper, pen, and a lot of guts, many women start their own secretarial businesses and contract out to several companies, particularly small businesses.

Elaine, an executive secretary for six years, says: "I got a good deal on a used computer and printer. I started moonlighting after hours at my old bosses' firm and gradually had enough of my own clients that I could leave my full-time job. I make $200 more a month, and I'm able to spend more time with my eighteen-month-old baby. I'm a much happier person to be around."

**Customer-Relations Representative**   Businesses say they have good relations with their customers, but most customers will tell you different. Startup equipment for a customer-relations business would be strong interpersonal skills and the ability to recognize customer dissatisfaction.

While working full-time as a doctor's assistant, Sylvia went back to school at night to take psychology and business classes. She changed careers to become a customer-relations representative for a health professionals company. "In the medical profession, patients are either happy or unhappy about their treatment. It's my job to keep the happy ones happy and to find the real reason behind an unhappy patient. I do this as an independent contractor."

**Housecleaner** Bingo! One of the main trends for the '90s is convenience and service. And, with over half the working population being female, you can bet there are a lot of houses out there that need cleaning. You don't like housework? That's OK. You keep the books and train your staff to do the cleaning. You think it's beneath you? My parents came to this country as immigrants after World War II. They were without family, money, or training. My mom cleaned houses, just to make ends meet. You would never believe my mom ever lifted a finger if you met her today.

The only start-up tools you'll need are cleaning supplies and good ol' elbow grease.

**Typesetter** Printing companies, artists, and advertising agencies often contract with independent typesetters. You don't even need your own computer. Mary, who typesets for two printers, works at a 24-hour copying shop that rents computers by the hour. "I bill my clients $9.50 an hour plus the direct cost of the rental. I stay busier than I would like sometimes."

**Graphic Artist** Businesses constantly develop and change logos, brochures, stationery, flyers, and other collateral material; need new designs for packaging; and require signs and other professional-looking graphics. If you have the training and experience, going into business for yourself could be the thing for you.

**Computer Consultant** Women who have had extensive computer training in their work and have been laid off, want more flexible hours, or want to make more money for themselves can offer their computer skills to temporary agencies and other businesses.

**Provider of Children's Parties**   Parents, preschools, and children's groups are always looking for ways to keep children entertained. What about developing fun and educational programs as a means of making money? Could you create a puppet show around the alphabet, for preschoolers? Or develop an environmental theme for children in grammar school? If your interests and experience are in music, dance, or art, you may have the skill to start your own kid-entertainment business.

All the businesses described here have a low start-up budget and require:

- Networking with other business people in related and unrelated fields
- Being involved in activities in the local business community
- Asking existing clients for new clients
- Becoming known in the community by participating in community organizations, functions, churches, and so on
- Servicing your existing clients on a continual basis
- Becoming a member of professional groups
- Marketing your business 365 days a year, every year

## Learn from Publications

The books and pamphlets that follow will be helpful if you are considering starting your own business.

*Employees: How to Find and Pay Them*, by the Small Business Administration. Washington, D.C.: Small Business Administration, Office of Business Development. This 18-page publication provides information about the basics: interviewing, pay, temporary services, and more.

*Entrepreneurial Woman's Guide to Owning a Business,* by Entrepreneur Magazine. Irvine, CA: Entrepreneur Group, Business Report Division, 1992. This guide provides self-evaluations and checklists for prospective female entrepreneurs. It discusses writing a business plan, creating an image, and distributing a product.

*Our Wildest Dreams: Women Entrepreneurs Making Money, Having Fun, Doing Good,* by Joline Godfrey. New York: Harper Business, a division of HarperCollins, 1992. This author shows that there are several ways to run a business, as well as to measure its success.

*Succeeding in Small Business: The 101 Toughest Problems and How to Solve Them,* by Jane Applegate. New York: NAL/Dutton, a division of Penguin USA, 1992. This book tells how to turn your skills into a business and describes the difficult problems the author and her clients have confronted.

*Understanding Cash Flow,* by the Small Business Administration. Washington, D.C.: Small Business Administration, Office of Business Development. This resource is a 10-page pamphlet that discusses the elements of cash flow.

*Your Small Business Made Simple,* by Richard Gallagher. New York: Doubleday, 1989. This is a workbook that takes you through the stages of running a business.

## Learn from Groups

The associations that follow can give you help and save you time.

- The Small Business Administration (SBA) offers many publications and programs that may be helpful. For example:

  The Demonstration Project Program: This program offers counseling and long-term training for women who are starting or expanding their businesses. Five thousand women have received this training to date.

The Service Corps of Retired Executives (SCORE): Through SCORE, retired executives volunteer their expertise for the benefit of new business owners.

Small Business Institutes:   The institutes are located on college campuses, where they perform market research and offer hands-on counseling for the owners of existing businesses. Graduate students in business departments perform these duties, often without a fee to the business owners.

Small Business Development Centers: These centers provide counseling, training, publications, and research assistance for small-business managers.

For more information on any of the SBA programs, write to the U.S. Small Business Administration, Office of Women's Business Ownership, 409 Third St. SW, Washington, D.C. 20416. To get the names of Small Business Development Centers, call (800) 633-6450.

- The National Association of Women Business Owners:   For more information about this group, write to the association's office at 600 South Federal St., Ste. 400, Chicago, IL 60605. The group's telephone number is (312) 922-0465.

- The National Federation of Independent Business: For information, phone (202) 554-9000.

## Nurture Your Business in an Incubator Office

The so-called incubator office, or office suite, is a business environment designed to help the owners of small businesses keep operating costs low. Incubator offices provide office space and access to basic business services, which all incubator occupants share. For example, owners of different businesses in an incubator office might share a receptionist, an answering service, a copier, a fax machine, and computers. Incubator office environments may be privately owned and run for profit or sponsored by a nonprofit group. Such nonprofit groups include economic development agencies, neighborhood revitalization groups, colleges, and chambers of commerce.

## *Share an Office*

To cut costs, find an office that pleases you and bring in one or two other people to share the space and the expenses. You don't need compatible personalities; you just need different schedules. One woman, a Traditional Homemaker, wanted to write. She wrote in the office in the mornings, while her children were in school. Another woman, also a Traditional Homemaker, wanted to paint. She put her daughter in afternoon kindergarten and painted at the office from 1:30 P.M. until 3:30. The third office partner, an Achieving Woman, worked full-time during the day as a college professor. After 6:00 P.M., she conducted a private therapy practice in the office the writer and the painter used during the day. This arrangement lasted for 3½ years.

## IMPORTANT POINTS TO REMEMBER

Job sharing or flextime may be the working woman's answer to the need for a more flexible work schedule. Other options for creating alternate work styles include working at home, increasing time off by arranging for comp time or personal days, buying a franchise, or starting your own business.

You are a prime candidate for a different employment style if you're exhausted daily, have constant bouts with viruses, are constantly irritable, wish for Friday on Monday, and get to bed past midnight just to keep up with housework.

Be creative when you evaluate your options. Decide on a flexible work schedule that works for you and do what you need to do to make it a reality.

# 7

# TAKING CONTROL OF YOUR SCHEDULE (BEFORE SOMEONE ELSE DOES)

---

Without plans, reflection, and careful judgment, most goals would never be accomplished, and our lives would be chaos. Without well-planned schedules, most days would be hectic, and our lives would feel out of control.

## USING A MONTHLY CALENDAR TO AVOID SCHEDULE OVERLOADS

With everything you need to do, it is no wonder that you tend to overload your schedule and often feel overwhelmed. Allowing time to prepare for deadlines, tracking heavily scheduled days, and staying aware of your energy level can help keep days manageable and well organized and help you develop a feeling of control. Remember, however, that an occasional crazy day is inevitable—when your child's last basketball game, your best friend's birthday party, and an important organizational meeting fall within 30 minutes of each other.

The best tool for avoiding schedule overloads is the month-at-a-glance calendar. There isn't much in life that is absolute. However, I am absolutely certain that it is time to throw away your daily or weekly calendar and replace it with a monthly one. The best size in terms of handling, flexibility, and functionality is approximately 8½ by 9 inches when closed; it opens to approximately 17 by 9 inches.

Other calendars are annoyances because they allow you to focus on only one day or week at a time. The monthly calendar allows the working woman to plan for and focus on a month at a time. Let's explore the advantages of the month-at-a-glance calendar more fully.

When using this calendar, the working woman doesn't need to shuffle pages back and forth to view the upcoming week. She can therefore plan any number of activities for the entire month.

By viewing the month-at-a-glance calendar, she can plan to keep the afternoon or entire day before a deadline clear of appointments so that she has enough time for last-minute preparations. In addition, with one glance, the working woman can decide to plan some downtime during a particularly busy week.

My eleven-year-old son was browsing through my month-at-a-glance calendar in my office one evening as he was waiting for me to help him learn his lines for *Snow White and the Seven Dwarfs*. He said, "Mom, you are very, very, very . . . " I thought he was going to say *busy*, but instead he finished the sentence this way: " . . . well organized." My eleven-year-old son is able to perceive the difference between being busy and well organized, and, once you start using a month-at-a-glance calendar, you will too—and will appreciate the change that difference makes in your life.

The first part of this chapter will discuss five ways for making the best use of your month-at-a-glance calendar:

- Take your calendar everywhere.
- Circle important dates in red.
- Keep time open before and after a trip.
- Divide each day into three parts.
- Schedule timeouts.

## Take Your Calendar Everywhere

Carry the following three items with you at all times, except social functions: your month-at-a-glance calendar; a notepad encased in a leather carrying case; and your business cards, preferably in a gold-plated card case.

The calendar tells others that you are organized and in control of your life, and it keeps you from overloading your schedule. The notepad says that you are responsible, and the business cards state that you are professional. Making such an impression is a surefire way to help you make career advances, both in the corporate world and in the small-business market.

## Circle Important Dates in Red

Circle in red the dates of deadlines, speeches, presentations, and similar activities. By distinguishing these dates clearly, you can keep from overloading yourself before and after them.

For example, if I have a speech scheduled for the 14th of a certain month, I circle the number "14" in red. I know that I should not plan appointments or out-of-town seminars for two full days before the speech and one full day after it.

The reason I plan my schedule this way is so that I have plenty of time to think, create, change, or modify my speech. When minor emergencies come up, which they inevitably do, I am in a much better frame of mind to take care of them. I keep the day after a speech clear because I need some downtime to rest and get re-energized. I have found that I love to give speeches, but they take a lot of energy.

I also circle important family dates—like my daughter's Bat Mitzvah, my children's opening-night theater performances, and all family members' birthdays—since I'm the one who usually prepares the accompanying parties.

## Keep Time Open Before and After a Trip

It's inevitable that the day before you leave town for a vacation, conference, or business trip, you try and cram a whole week's worth of work into one day. I think it's the working woman's code of ethics.

After all, you have wash to do, the house needs to be cleaned, the children's lunches made, and all your papers filed. Such directives come from the same area in the brain that says you have to clean the house before the cleaning lady comes.

Keep the day before your trip clear so that you can take care of last-minute details. No matter how well you plan your time, last-minute tasks will crop up both at work and at home. To think this won't happen only sets you up for last-minute pressures, a big headache at the end of the day, and second thoughts about leaving.

Also, keep the day of your return and the day after it free. This will allow you to take care of business at hand, and it will help you ease into the flow of events. Sharon, an accountant, does not plan any appointments the day she returns to the office. "The only thing I plan on my return to the office after being gone for more than one day, is to open mail and return calls from the days I was not in the office. I don't attend my regularly scheduled Rotary meeting if it lands on the same day as my first day into the office. Somehow, the interruption of the meeting gets me further off kilter.

"When I learned I wasn't going to complete anything that first day I'm back, I started to relax and take the day more casually. The funny thing is . . . I started getting more accomplished just by opening and filing my mail and returning all my calls. At the end of the day, I feel as though I have accomplished a lot."

## Divide Each Day into Three Parts

Take each day space on the calendar and mentally divide it into three imaginary parts: upper third, middle third, and lower third. The upper third of the calendar space is for noting appointments that occur any time from 7:00 A.M. to noon. The middle third is for noting appointments from noon to 4:30 P.M. The lower third calendar space is for noting appointments from 4:30 through the evening.

By dividing the day into thirds, the working woman can quickly view her day and determine if she has a heavy morning, afternoon, or evening. This information will help determine if she should schedule more appointments or time for quiet concentration. If I have a busy afternoon (that is, if the middle third of the calendar space is crowded), then I try to keep my mornings clear so that I have time to do what needs to be done in the office.

Libby, a human resources specialist, plans to see her clients in the afternoon. She spends the morning preparing for appointments and doing any other office work she needs to do. She also keeps Monday, Wednesday, and Friday evenings clear for her family. "I just need to take a quick glance at my calendar to know if I should schedule something in on a certain day or wait until another day to make the appointment or lunch date. This is especially helpful when I'm on the phone. I can give an answer about a certain date or time within seconds of looking at my calendar."

## Schedule Timeouts

A marketing consultant and part-time writer schedules
from 11:45 A.M. to 1:30 P.M. as a timeout for herself. "I
used to go out to lunch with friends and clients. I now
get together with friends in the evening and clients at
breakfast. I schedule an occasional lunch with clients that
can't make any other time. Blocking out the time on my
calendar between 11:45 and 1:30 gives me a chance to exercise, shower, and dress in the same amount of time that
I used to have lunch appointments. After eating lunch,
I used to feel sluggish. Now, I am completely refreshed,
and I am ready to go when I get to my office."

Let's pull together all the tips presented so far in this
chapter:

- Buy a month-at-a-glance calendar.
- Take the calendar wherever you go, except social
  functions.
- Take a notepad to all business functions.
- Always have business cards with you.
- Keep the day before and the day after a trip un-
  planned.
- Divide each calendar day into imaginary thirds.
  Note morning appointments in the upper third of
  the space, afternoon appointments in the middle
  third, and evening appointments in the lower third.
- Start *now*!

By looking at her calendar the working woman can tell
how she spends her time and if the time mix is compatible
with her motivational style. She can also determine if the
day, week, or month was used to bring her closer to her
goals or if her activities took her further away from them.

Let's go through the steps to determine if you are
reaching your goals or if you are spending most of your
time on busywork.

## USING YOUR CALENDAR TO BALANCE YOUR TIME

When a working woman sees how she is spending her time, she may well be motivated to change her time use. Based on this theory, I have developed a method of time analysis that uses a calendar and colors. The only necessary equipment is your month-at-a-glance calendar and three colored pencils or pens—yellow, green, and red. Here's how it works.

**Professionally Speaking**   First, go through the last week and underline, in yellow, all notations about activities that led you in a positive direction professionally. For example, underline notations about preparing for a presentation, a meeting for breakfast or lunch with a client or prospective client, reading up on a professional topic, meeting with staff starting a project, or planning time.

**On the Home Front**   Underline, in green, all notations about activities related to home goals. These would include notes about calling a cleaning service to clean your home, starting a laundry assembly line at home with other family members, visiting a child's teacher, going to lunch with a family member, taking a child to the doctor for a six-month checkup, or anything that keeps you in tune with your family life.

**On the Personal Side**   Finally, underline in red all the weekly activities that helped you get closer to your personal goals: notes about exercise; a timeout; a visit with friends; or massage, manicure, or hair appointments.

### Restructure Your Time to Fit Your Personality

When she analyzed her calendar, Sarah, an attorney and an Achieving Woman, found that she was spending more time on home activities than on personal areas. "I knew I felt completely overwhelmed; I was staying at the office late at night and worked almost all weekends just to maintain at work. I feel like a rag doll each morning. After I analyzed where my time was going, I did something about it. I hired a courier service to do all my home errands. Someone from the service returns an unwanted gift, pays an over-due bill in person, or delivers personal gifts. I don't know why I didn't think of this earlier, because our firm uses a courier to take and pick up legal briefs all the time. It's far less expensive than the time it would take me to do it.

"I also set up a carpool system with my children's friends' parents. They take and I pick up from soccer and basketball practice. I still try to make as many games as I can. I now get weekly massages . . . it's less expensive in money and time and more effective than the chiroprac-tor. Plus, it feels better."

Sarah recently analyzed her calendar again and found that she is now spending far less time on home errands. She works in the office only one day each weekend, she spends time with her family on Sundays, and she has started an exercise program—she walks every morning. "I still have a lot to do, but I don't feel as ragged or angry. I can't believe what a little restructuring can do."

By analyzing her calendar, Jeanie, a Traditional Home-maker with four active children, found that she was spend-ing almost 85% of her time on the home front but had very little personal time. "I gave up baking cookies for each classroom party. That was really hard—my children don't care, but I liked doing it because the house smelled so good. It's the same smell that I remember from when I was growing up, but my mom says she would *never* chauf-feur her children around the way I do. No wonder she always had the time to bake."

Kristan, a Transitional Woman, found she spent most of her time working. "I used to take work home almost every night and got the children in bed as quickly as I could so I could finish my office job. I usually ended up feeling frustrated because I couldn't spend enough time with my family."

Twelve weeks after analyzing her activities, Kristan accepted a lateral career move that required less responsibility and fewer after-hour meetings. "I still work a lot, but I don't have to rush my kids to bed anymore. I spend 10 to 15 minutes with each child (two) at bedtime. I wish I had more time with them, but this is an enjoyable time for all of us. We all have warmer feelings towards each other, and there's not nearly as much fussing."

## IMPORTANT POINTS TO REMEMBER

There are several ways to avoid overloading your schedule. Use a month-at-a-glance calendar. With one glance you can decide to plan downtime during a particularly busy week. A month-at-a-glance calendar keeps you well organized rather than busy.

Take your calendar everywhere (except dressy social functions). Circle important dates in red. This signals the need to schedule time between activities.

Keep the day before and after a trip unplanned. This helps ease your schedule and lowers your anxiety. Divide each day of your calendar into three imaginary parts: morning, afternoon, and evening. Write appointment times in the appropriate space so the calendar can give you a visual signal to warn you about over- or underbooking.

Block out time, in advance, to use for personal activities. And, most important, find out where you're spending time by analyzing your calendar. You will feel in control when your schedule fits your personality and lifestyle. It's worth the effort.

# 8

# BEATING STRESS BY BREAKING THE RULES

Stress is responsible for a myriad of problems ranging from depression to headaches to a sagging libido. In addition to an overloaded schedule, boredom ranks high on the list of the symptoms of stress.

It never hurts to fight stress with a little healthy "rebellion" once in a while. By rebellion I simply mean doing something that represents a distinct break from your regular schedule. As an employee or employer, build up a store of compensatory time, or "comp" time—that is, time off that you take without pay to compensate you for extra time spent at work. A store of comp time will allow you to take occasional mental-health days. You could use your afternoon off to catch a matinee or special sale, enjoy a midweek romantic getaway with a lover, or take a class that teaches belly dancing or the art of striptease.

After interviewing hundreds of women over the years, I have come to the conclusion that 80% of stress comes from self-induced time-pressures: by being late because of poor scheduling, by not allowing enough time to complete work or pursue personal interests, and by not allowing enough time to spend with family and friends.

The other 20% is "good" stress. Experts agree that

good stress—which arises from the right amount of challenge—can increase your energy level, productivity, and
creativity. The optimum amount of stress is different for
each person.

## How to Spend Time to Save Time

It's easy for working women to overdo and overcommit.
When you feel overwhelmed and stressed, your body
stops working properly. It goes into overdrive and shuts
down creativity. Physiologically, our bodies cannot work
properly under extreme stress and tension. It is as worth-
less to spend hours working on a project, without a rest,
as it is to work under tension. In both cases, you waste
time and spin your wheels. Certainly, you have worked on
a project with a bad tension headache and realized the
next day that your work was far from good or properly
completed.

In these instances, it would have been far wiser—in
time, expense, and professional self-esteem—to walk away
from the task at hand and walk around the block, do 20
jumping jacks, or leave for the afternoon.

In other words, you need to *spend* time on yourself in
order to save time on your task. Here are several more suggestions for going about this:

- Take half a day or a full day off when you're feeling
  overwhelmed. As long as you find a replacement
  and get your work completed, most employers do
  not mind. Be honest, tell him or her you need a
  mental-health day. Make sure this does not happen
  too often.

  Joann asked for a "personal" day off two days after
  returning from a business trip. "I just needed some
  time to catch my breath. I felt overwhelmed and

lost. I slept in until 8:30 A.M., took a long bath, and just stayed home. That one day off recharged my energy level."

- Leave the office when you are feeling stressed. Staying in a stressful situation without any relief only exacerbates the situation. Take a walk, listen to relaxing music for 10 minutes with your eyes shut. Think of pleasant thoughts.

  Susan, a medical doctor, takes at least 30 minutes at the end of the day to "just sit and change gears from work to home. When I enter the door to my home, I try and keep all of the office activities out of my head. Besides being a doctor, I'm also a mom."

- If you're a morning person, wake up an hour earlier every morning; if you're a night person, stay up an hour later. Meditate, listen to music, read the paper with a cup of tea or coffee, take a walk, or do anything else that is completely for *you* and is stress reducing.

  Janet wakes up at 5:30 A.M. so that she can read the paper and sip a cup of coffee before she wakes the rest of the household. Also, she spends some of this time reading meditative commentary. "This time in the morning is my favorite time of day. It gives me a reference point for the rest of the day. It helps give me faith that what I plan to accomplish each day is worthwhile and has a purpose."

## LONG-TERM STRESS VERSUS SHORT-TERM STRESS

Our physiology is such that, in the face of danger, our hormonal level changes so we can either fight or flee in an instant. Being in this state for extended periods is dangerous because it causes the immune system to work overtime and, eventually, break down.

Medical researchers and doctors believe that this breakdown of the immune system is the culprit in many illnesses: certain types of cancer, gastrointestinal problems, skin irritations, recurring viruses, arthritis, migraine headaches, and more.

It is far easier, healthier, and less expensive to take the time and reverse the situations that cause you stress than to try to work in spite of them.

I know that the urge to continue working can be strong, even though you know your productivity is dwindling. As I sit here writing this chapter, I have an intense urge to continue writing—even though my back is giving out and my cold is getting worse. How do I go about leaving my work for tomorrow when I really want to ignore my body and keep going?

I talk to myself and say, Stop what you're doing, you're on work overload. *Stop!* (It works, honest!)

## Traditional Stress-Busters

Stress-busters are activities you can undertake to stop the upward spiral of stress. The three traditional stress-busters are:

- A hot bath
- Window-shopping
- Exercise

**Take a Hot Bath**    Almost every evening I dim the bathroom lights, lock my bedroom and bathroom door, light a fragrance candle, and take a hot bath with Epsom salt. My family knows this is my quiet time and that I am not to be disturbed. I'm in the bathtub for at least 20 minutes, and I immerse my entire body up to my neck. I consciously let go of anything negative that happened during the day and try hard not to think about anything special. This sets the stage for a peaceful night's rest.

**Window-Shop**    Carrie stays home and takes care of three children. I asked her how she keeps the stress down. "My husband will come home during lunch, and I will go out and window-shop. I love to look at window displays and the color combinations they use. I also know what styles are coming up. It's like reading a fashion magazine on a large three-dimensional scale. If my husband can't come home, I hire a babysitter for 2 hours."

**Exercise**    Janet sits at her desk most of the day. Stress from sitting as well as managing 25 people in her department can take its toll. Janet handles stress by walking around her building several times a day. "It's become a joke. When someone is trying to reach me by phone and I can't be found, my secretary says 'she's strolling the grounds.' I started walking by happenstance. A co-worker and I had some extra time at lunch before going back to the office, and we decided to walk around the block. I remember feeling so good after doing this that I kept it up. Now you can find me putting on my tennis shoes and walking downstairs several times a day."

## Creative Stress-Busters

In addition to the traditional stress-busters, consider the tips in the list that follows. Each suggestion involves activity that is more mental than physical and may call for creativity or an attitude change.

- Change the situation.
- Let go!
- Learn to live with what you cannot change.
- Take time to play.
- Trust your intuition and decisions.
- Use weekends to re-energize and build fond memories.

- Be patient.
- Live now.
- Avoid labeling.
- Stay positive.
- Examine your choices.

**Change the Situation**  In many cases, you do not have the power to make decisions that will change policy, co-workers, or anything else. However, there are situations that you can change or modify by developing and substantiating your ideas. This is not an easy way to make changes, but patience and persistence are the key.

Eleanor worked in the accounting department at an engineering firm for two years. She found a particular procedure most stressful. "I told the head accountant that we backtrack using this particular form, but the company did nothing. I then took the matter into my own hands. I revised the form to my specifications and turned it in. The head accountant asked, 'What the hell is this?' After I showed him how it works, he said we could try it if everyone wanted to." With a smile Eleanor said, "Two weeks later everyone in the department was using the E-form." (E for *Eleanor.*)

**Let Go!**  Letting go of negative thoughts is not an easy task by anyone's standards. Laura, a Transitional Woman, has a difficult time leaving the house messy in the morning. "There's no way I can get the kids off to school and be at the office by 8 A.M. and keep my house tidy. Every morning I got angry with the kids on the way to school. I arrived at the office grumpy. I finally decided to just let the house go. Now, the kids straighten up while I make dinner. We're all a lot happier," smiles Laura. "I learned that the kids and my husband didn't care about the untidy house; I did. I'm still a good person even if my dishes are in the sink and washed clothes are sitting on the sofa in the front room."

**Learn to Live with What You Cannot Change**  There are times when nothing you do can change or modify a situation. Nancy is a full-time mom with four children. She has rheumatoid arthritis and never knows when her shoulder or leg joints will give out. She would like to go to work outside the home, but doesn't know exactly what to do. Because her husband is seldom home, all child-care responsibilities lie with her. "I can't think about 'what if,' because I'm too busy doing what I have to do. But I'm going to go back to school when the baby is in preschool. I will then take different classes to determine what field I like. I know I can't make any changes now, but it doesn't mean I can't plan for the future."

**Take Time to Play**   The Traditional Homemaker feels she must spend playtime with the family, not in playing to benefit only herself. The Transitional Woman feels she can't take time to play, because there just isn't any time left between work and family responsibilities.

The Achieving Woman feels she needs to be doing something all the time and that the something needs to have a purpose. She views "unproductive" time as wasted.

The Traditional Homemaker needs to set aside time when the children are at school or napping. She can spend that time taking a relaxing bath, reading, working in the garden (if she enjoys it), or doing anything else that relaxes her. The Transitional Woman needs to tell herself she deserves some time off just for herself. When she is less stressed, the entire family will be less stressed. The Achieving Woman must realize that taking the time to play and re-energize will make her *more* productive in the long run. Her creative juices will flow better when she is relaxed. She must learn that to relax is not wasteful and to incorporate this fact into her belief system.

**Trust Your Intuition and Decisions**   I feel that a woman's intuition is one of her strongest attributes. A woman's intuition is the final jury to most good decisions. Never trust someone else's choices if you feel they are not for you. Jon Kabat-Zinn, Ph.D, author of *Full Catastrophe Living*, says:

"Trust your intuition and your own authority, even if you make some mistakes along the way. Then, you get into the habit of looking inside yourself for guidance. If something doesn't feel right to you, honor your feelings."

**Use Weekends to Re-Energize and Build Fond Memories**
Traditional Homemakers feel that weekends are for family get-togethers. However, watching soccer and baseball games, unless you truly enjoy them, are not re-energizing activities. To re-energize herself, Nancy tries to go on a family picnic one weekend day each week. "I enjoy watching the kids play in the park. I'm away from the house so I can't do any housework. It's definitely a special time for me and the kids."

Transitional Women feel that weekends are for errands. Now that Janet has learned to use weekends for rejuvenation, she takes Saturday completely off. "I sleep in till 8 A.M., lounge around the house playing with plants or reading the paper. Each child may ask a friend over Saturdays after 12 P.M., or they can go over to a friend's house. The only stipulation is that they need to get their own rides—the chauffeur is not available on Saturdays, only Sunday through Friday."

Achieving Women feel that weekends are for getting more work done. The trick is to get these women relaxed and show them how positive relaxation is for the body and mind.

I was working seven days a week, five on marketing and public relations and two on writing. Any way you cut it, it came out to seven days a week. I justified this intense body and mind workout because of my writing deadlines. As a result of my weekend work marathons, I found that I was not as creative on Monday, my brainstorming day, nor was I feeling physically relaxed.

I now take Friday night and Saturdays off. I sleep in and then go out to breakfast *by myself*; read the paper; and come home 1½ hours later, feeling extremely refreshed.

In my absence, my husband takes our oldest son to his soccer game (I am soccered out after seven years) and our other two children, ages fourteen and nine, sleep or watch TV. After my excursion, I'm mentally prepared to do things with the family. I like the outdoors, so we may play basketball in our driveway or play tennis. It's a great feeling not to be anywhere at any time and let the mood, not the clock, determine what to do next!

**Be Patient** People and events unfold in their own time. Most things in life occur with time, persistence, and a focus. Our fast-paced society in conjunction with new technological advances—such as fax machines, modems, faster computers and printers, and car phones—cause more stress and keep us from learning to be patient. Losing weight, done properly, takes time. After you start weight lifting, it takes time before you see muscle definition.

My impatience to get things done drove me to lengthen my work day by making 7 A.M. breakfast meetings. I was consistently working 11-hour days. I could feel the long hours bringing down my immunity. This became especially clear when I developed an inner-ear imbalance that affected my equilibrium and made me dizzy. I thought I had brain cancer. My body was giving me a clear signal about the error of my impatient ways. Even after I made the decision to sleep more, walk in the mornings, and set up only two early breakfast meetings a week, it took me three weeks to make the goal a reality.

According to Jon Kabat-Zinn, "to be patient is simply to be completely open to each moment, accepting it in its fullness, knowing that, like the butterfly, things can unfold only in their own time."

**Live Now** The only time you *really* have is *now*. It is important to be aware of what is going on around you at each moment. As I sit here writing under a deadline, I am aware of the luscious greenery outside, my healthy family, and the dirty house I call home. Somehow the deadline is not as pressing or as important.

Ann lived in the fast lane, as far as her job was concerned. She traveled over a week each month on business-related meetings, worked hard on making a second marriage with stepchildren work, and planned to start her own business in the future. When I visited with Ann concerning the development of seminars, we would quickly get our work done and share secrets about the future.

Not long after she had shared an idea for a new business with me, she was hospitalized and diagnosed with liver cancer. She was one of those positive types who flew out of town for treatments and kept planning her future. Nine months later, she left me with fond memories and her grandchildren with two dollhouses she had made from scratch. Her company hired three people to do the work Ann had done. I often think of her and wonder if she would have started her new business if she could have seen into the future.

In other words, the future is uncertain, the past is over, and the only real thing we have is *now*. This concept helps keep priorities in shape. It helps you stay aware of your surroundings and of what is truly important today.

Jon Kabat-Zinn says it best: "Awareness, insight and health will ripen if you pay attention to and honor all the moments you live."

**Avoid Labeling**   It is very easy to label yourself, other people, and actions as good or bad. This attitude can be self-defeating. "I would go through the whole day saying how 'good' or 'bad' things were. If I missed a backup case at work, I would say how bad things were," comments Tracey, a court reporter. "I started to become aware of what I said to myself . . . and was amazed. So much of what I saw was negative, from the behavior of my two-year-old daughter to what my boyfriend wore at social gatherings. I work very hard at being less judgmental. It not only causes me less tension, but my relationship with my daughter and boyfriend have improved."

**Stay Positive** Staying positive under stress and time-pressures is easier said than done. It takes a conscious effort to think positively.

Susan, the doctor, says: "I have three choices on how I deal with a situation that doesn't go the way I expect: I can be upset, smile, or walk away. In most cases I choose to smile. Quite honestly, it takes less effort."

**Examine Your Choices** Let's look at some choices a woman named Laura has in regard to working and keeping her home tidy. "I went through all the choices. I could stay home, have a clean house, and no money. I could hire a cleaning lady, but then the house would only be clean for one or two days afterwards. (I tried this for four years.) I could work part-time, but I couldn't find a good-paying job part-time. Or, I could go to work at a job I liked and not look back when I left in the mornings. After considering all my choices, I picked the last one."

## Low-Cost Tips for Re-Establishing Yourself

The old cliché "A stitch in time saves nine" can be converted to a working woman's cliché: "Taking personal time saves you money and stress down the line."

You may have noticed a common theme in the traditional stress-busting tips and the stress-busters that take creativity. The common theme is take time for yourself. In the midst of all you have to accomplish, do things to remind yourself that you are more than a task-accomplishing machine; re-establish yourself as a human being. This can mean taking an action that frees you to do something you enjoy or giving yourself a treat. Taking time to re-establish yourself doesn't necessarily mean spending a lot of money. And, as we have discussed, what little you do spend will be a good investment in terms of your health and productivity.

The list that follows presents tips for re-establishing yourself. In many ways, I consider these actions musts for saving self and money.

- Treat yourself to a house helper at least once a month. This house helper can be your sitter, a teen-ager, or a janitorial service. Go for whatever your priorities and budget will allow. (Figured in terms of your hourly wage, hiring help will probably be cheaper than hiring yourself to do the same work.)
- Treat yourself to a gardener at least once a month. (It's cheaper than going to the doctor with back pains.) Again, the gardener can be a teenager or a friend who needs a little extra money.
- Treat yourself to pretty undergarments once in a while. (They're cheaper than a whole new outfit.)
- Treat yourself to a minimum of one hour per week of playtime. (It's cheaper than taking sick leave from work.)
- Treat yourself to new lipstick. (It's cheaper than a complete makeover.)
- Treat yourself to a new pair of earrings or a scarf. (It's cheaper than an outfit or shoes.)
- Treat yourself to an at-home hair-conditioning program. (It takes less time to condition your hair than to cut it off and wait for it to grow back.)
- Treat yourself by taking one day at a time, *positively*. (It's cheaper than being tied up with a tension headache.)
- Treat yourself kindly, the way you want others to treat you. (Respect begets respect.)

## IMPORTANT POINTS TO REMEMBER

Most stress comes from self-induced time-pressures that result from poor scheduling. Part of effective time management is the realization that you need to spend time on yourself in order to save time on tasks. Listen to your body for stress signals and respond to them. To decrease stress, change the situation, if possible; let go of negative thoughts; learn to live with the things you cannot change; learn to take time to play; trust your intuition and decisions; use weekends for re-energizing and building fond memories; be patient; live *now*; avoid labeling; stay positive; and decide on choices.

# 9

# CRISIS AND CHALLENGE: OPPORTUNITIES FOR GROWTH

There is no such thing as a life without crises and challenges; how we *respond* to them is what makes the difference. By taking a positive rather than a negative approach, even the most formidable disasters and tasks can often be countered by a vital thrust in a new direction.

Crises, mistakes, and misdirection are not fatal. Indeed, much good can come of them if only we can respond constructively. The key to responding constructively is staying flexible—that is, not letting the temporary setback freeze us into inaction or despair. To do this, we must be able to distinguish the problem from our perception of the problem. This chapter will suggest ideas, attitude changes, and techniques that can help turn what looks like a negative situation into a positive one.

## RECOVERING FROM MISTAKES

Mundane and transient snafus such as having two appointments (or lovers) booked for the same time, missing a flight, staining a suit at a critical moment, forgetting the name of an important person, inadvertently hurting someone's feelings, and handling minor rejections *can* have a noncrisis ending. Everyday snafus and mistakes can turn into learning experiences and opportunities.

Bobbie has a very busy family therapy practice. "I once scheduled a husband and wife going through a divorce at my office at the same time. Both parties still felt wounded and vulnerable. I apologized for my gross negligence. We started laughing in the waiting room. Believe it or not, my 'mistake' was a turning point for them therapeutically. They stopped seeing each other as monsters."

Like Bobbie, Krista was able to profit from a mistake. "I went out to lunch with a new client and his girlfriend. Two people at different times walked up to the table to say hi to me. I introduced my client but forgot his girl-friend's name both times. I apologized and we laughed it off. I used this awkward situation as a funny way to open my conversations with my client. I'd call him and say, 'Hi, this is Krista. What was your name again?' To this day, I can't remember her name."

## Confront the "Whoops!"

Mistakes happen! In fact, I guarantee that you will have to pay taxes; make mistakes; and, eventually, die.

Most situations can be fixed after a mistake. We do damage when the mistake goes on for a long time—when we do not confront it or take action to correct it.

Apologize, but do not feel indebted for the rest of your life. There's an old Jewish proverb: "Don't waste good agony."

Different types of women react differently to their own mistakes. The Traditional Homemaker feels especially upset by her mistakes, since she believes that she should

know better or that her female counterpart who works outside the home wouldn't have let the mistake happen. The
Transitional Woman feels guilty about making mistakes,
often thinking that, if she weren't so torn between all the
hats she wears, mistakes would not happen. The Achieving
Woman moves ahead fast, without taking many breaths
in between activities. She knows that mistakes will happen, and she takes action when they do.

## Go with the Flow

All women must learn to go with the flow when mistakes
happen. Rather than perceiving a mistake as a monstrous
catastrophe, accept it and go on. It is common for women
to dwell on their mistakes and view them as failures. Janet
says, "I know I'm going a mile a minute, if not faster, and
I know that I am going to make some mistakes . . . big ones
and little ones. I have to remember to look at my mistakes,
not as failures, but as growth . . . it sure is hard to do
sometimes."

Nelson Boswell said "The difference between greatness
and mediocrity is often how an individual views a mistake. . . . " Sarah, a friend of mine, has a propensity for
snagging her hose or staining her clothes at critical moments. "I feel horrible when I do this. I think everyone
is looking at me and thinking What a slob. I have a high-
profile career, and it's necessary to look presentable at all
times. . . . I don't have a lot of extra suits to bring to the
office. Anyway, I would need to change shoes, hose, and
whatever. Instead, I find that it takes far less space and
is a lot cheaper to buy pins and stick 'em on the stains.
I have little ones and large ones with silver and gold
backgrounds. I laugh inside when someone comments on
my pins or tells me how together I look." Sarah adds a
whole new meaning to the concept of dressing fashionably!

## FREEING OURSELVES FROM MISPERCEPTIONS

Facing a crisis or meeting a challenge may take all the energy we have. Yet many of us sap our energy by worrying, being angry or impatient, or avoiding the problem. To avoid wasting energy in this way, incorporate these ideas into your approach:

- Think of time as a neutral concept.
- Avoid "should-driven" behavior.
- Take action despite your perceptions of the situation.

### *Think of Time as a Neutral Concept*

Time, or at least the concept of time, is neutral. Time begins to have meaning because of our frame of mind. Cathie, a stockbroker, discusses how the context affects her perception of time. "On vacation, time may revolve around naps and 'what are we doing for dinner?' questions. I seem to be obsessed with what I'm eating at mealtimes when I'm on vacation, but don't have that need when I'm home working.

"When I'm reading a novel, I lose all concept of time, but when I'm up against a deadline, it seems my heart beats with the tick of the clock. I can't believe how slowly time goes by when I'm waiting for a question to be answered, and how fast it goes when I'm working on a project."

When you're waiting at a doctor's office or waiting for a client, time takes on new perceived value. We look at these situations as "time-pressures" or "time-wasters" that bring stress into our lives. If we can just remember that time, in itself, has no value, we can avoid wasting energy on being emotional about our perceptions.

## Avoid "Should-Driven" Behavior

If allowed, women let their feelings of "should" and "should not" govern their behavior. The Traditional Home-maker feels she "should" be preparing home-cooked meals, since she doesn't "work" and has so much "free" time. The Transitional Woman feels she has too much to do but "should" still be an ever-attentive wife and mother. The Achieving Woman feels that, to reach her goals, she "should" be more involved in work and home functions.

Should-driven behavior is another energy waster. If a goal is not important to *you*, then do not let it haunt you. Do not let other people's values, or your perception of them, determine how you use your resources.

## Take Action Despite Perceptions

This step is the second part of freeing yourself from should-driven behavior. Suppose you determine that you are being haunted by a "should." Furthermore, suppose you determine that the "should" is attached to a goal that you'd like to accomplish but that seems out of your reach. The key, at this point, is to take action despite your percep-tion of the impossibility of the task.

This philosophy is part of the New Action-Oriented Therapy, which was developed by Japanese therapists Mirita and Naikan. They claim that taking action despite your perceptions of a situation helps you get done what you want to get done. A typical conversation with a New Action-Oriented therapist might go something like this:

"I really should spend more time working on reports."

"No, just do it."

"I need to make more of a commitment to spend time with my family and friends."

"No, just do it."

"I should be able to organize my life better."

"No, just do it."

You get the idea. The Japanese therapists suggest that, through discipline and a pragmatic approach to life, a person can address deep-seated inner feelings and achieve goals.

## Understanding Our Behavior

The way we perceive our time-pressures is a product of our values, both individually and socially. Since these perceptions are deeply rooted in our past and culture, they may be difficult to track down. In other words, it may be hard to understand why we're reacting to a problem the way we are. Once we understand ourselves, it is often easier to abandon unproductive approaches and try new ones that will work.

To help women understand their reactions to crises and challenges, I suggest an analysis I call the feel it—behave it approach. The woman divides a page of a yellow legal pad into two columns. At the top of the left-hand column, she writes "Feelings"; at the top of the right-hand column, she writes "Behavior." Linda, a dining-room hostess for a resort hotel, tried the analysis and found that it helped her discover why she was having trouble achieving her goal of spending more time with her children.

"I found that I didn't want to spend time with my older children, because, under the 'Feelings' column, I wrote: 'They are always talking about themselves, and when I say something about my day, they seem uninterested.' I feel neglected at home."

Under "Behavior" Linda wrote: "I don't mind the extra-long hours I spend at work. I'd rather be working. When I work I feel better because people listen to me. I'm somebody."

Linda recognized and accepted what she was doing and started taking the time to speak and have enjoyable time with each child once a day. She found that, when she gave her undivided attention to her teens, then they would do the same for her. "Now that I see why I was avoiding them, we now have some of our best talks."

Ginny wants a job with more responsibility, but she does not go on any job interviews. She was asked to interview with two companies, but she declined both requests. When she analyzed her behavior by using the feel it—behave it approach, her two columns looked like this:

| *Feelings* | *Behavior* |
|---|---|
| I am bored by my job. I am afraid that more responsibility at work would mean longer hours away from my family. A new job would mean I wouldn't have any time with them. | I find excuses for not going to job interviews even though they could lead to more money and the chance to use my skills. |

Think of an uncomfortable situation that you would like to change. Write the problem at the top of the page. Under "Feelings," write down your feelings in the situation. Are you angry, disgusted, bored, guilty, fearful, ambivalent, rejected, neglected? Write down all your emotions. Under "Behavior," write down your actual behavior in this specific situation—what you actually do or don't do. Perhaps you want to organize time better but say yes to everyone. Perhaps you want to start a family, but it's never the "right" time.

You will find that the way you feel has a direct impact on the way you behave.

## LIVING IN THE PRESENT

Living in the present rather than living in the past helps to keep life issues in perspective. When our perceptions are kept within the confines of a reality check, then the concept of time remains neutral and we can use our energy constructively.

## Use Reality Checks to Maintain Perspective

When we're in the mood for rock music, we turn the radio dial to a rock station. When we're in the mood for classical music, we know to turn the dial to that kind of station. If we are in the mood for oldies, we need to turn the dial again.

When we're in a crisis situation, we must use a reality check to turn the dial on our thoughts. A reality check can change negative and anxious thoughts into positive thoughts.

Dana took a day off to spend time with her father, who was recuperating from a routine hospital procedure. "When I first arrived at the hospital, I felt rushed, nervous, and frustrated that my dad chose that day for the exam. By midafternoon I needed to get out of this depressing place. I realized how fortunate I was to be able to walk out of here at any time. I don't *have* to be here because of a medical problem. Whenever I have a crisis situation, I just remember how closed in and depressing the hospital was, and I snap out of it."

"I remember when my little one had the croup," says Cindy, a medical assistant. "The doctor told me that children with croup sound worse than they are, but it can be dangerous. I have never heard anything so wretched in my life. I told myself that, if he gets better, I will never take anything but life-and-death issues so seriously again. It's been a year now, and I've *almost* kept my promise."

In times of crisis, use the points that follow as reality checks.

  • Ask yourself, What is the worst thing that can happen? If the answer is not a life-or-death matter, turn the dial. Turning the dial keeps your perspective in the present, the here and now.

- Immediately think of two of life's blessings. When you feel a slight smile on your face, you'll know you have turned the dial.

- Ask, Can this "crisis" turn into learning? If the answer is yes, turn the dial.

- Ask, Will time make things better? If the answer is yes, turn the dial. Even the most tragic of cases eventually gets better with time.

- If the "crisis" helps you feel humble, turn the dial. Golda Meir, Israel's fourth prime minister, said: "Don't be humble, you're not that great."

## PLANNING LIFE AS A WHOLE

If you look at a clock, you see that the face is divided into 12 major and 60 minor parts. It is the perception of these parts that makes some women obsessed with time. The obsession causes stress. Remember, the whole is greater than the sum of its ticking.

Rather than looking at time in increments—15 minutes, for example—look at time as a whole: a whole life. When you have only 30 minutes to complete the errands, the task becomes stressful. If the errands have not been done as part of a whole life, they take on a whole different perspective.

Susan Helper, a medical doctor, says: "I only have so many hours in my day. I have to divide these precious hours with my practice, my family, and my friends. If I look at each day and what I need to accomplish, I would go off the deep end. I try to keep my life in balance by not worrying if I don't accomplish everything today, because in the scheme of things I have longer than 24 hours to do it all."

I asked Susan what happens when she has to go to the hospital to see a patient and her son wants to read to her. "I obviously have to take care of my patient, not because the patient is more important than my children, but because the patient needs me right now. I feel it's important for children to know that they can't decide when they do and do not want to be with their parents. It's realistic to teach them that you can't have what you want when you want it at all times, and that they have to give something up once in a while also.

"It is important to plan life as a whole, rather than plan time with every click of the clock. The real question becomes What do you want to do with your life—what do you want to accomplish as a whole?" Susan wants to be an excellent medical doctor and to enjoy the other parts of her life—husband, children, friends. Looking at the whole helps her to put daily tasks in proper perspective. It can do the same for you and allow you to claim the lifestyle you *want*, rather than the tasks you have to do.

Two techniques can help you look at time and life as a whole:

- Ask yourself, Is it absolutely necessary to do this *now*?
- Make a daily to-do list.

## Ask If It Is Absolutely Necessary Now

Lorraine is the owner of a small business. She must take care of the business and her family each day. "Some days my list of things to do is so long it depresses me. I start out motivated, but usually I can't finish it all in one day. I keep asking myself if I *have* to do this now, or can it wait for later in the day or possibly the next day? I still get a lot done, but not everything I want to. I have learned to distinguish between what I have to do *now* and what I can do later."

## Make a Daily To-Do List

To make a to-do list, use one or two sheets of a legal pad. At the top of the sheet, write the day and date. At the top left margin, under the date, write "People to Call." Include phone numbers in *front* of the names. One of the biggest deterrents to making or returning calls quickly is having to look up the numbers.

About one third down the sheet, write "Things to Do." This is where you list what needs to be done for work, home, or yourself. Write the due date in front of your task. This helps you see its immediacy.

In the last third of the page, write "Places to Go." List the destinations in order. But be flexible—number 5 may become number 1 tomorrow. Number 4 may become number 2 because it's closer to the last stop than you previously thought.

Your to-do list should look something like this:

### DAILY TO-DO LIST

Wednesday, March 11, 2000

*People to Call:*

324-4687—Jim Drake/Oilfield Services/seminar update

323-4241—Carla Clips/Maintenance of office

800-336-1233—Reservation for the weekend of March 23–24

*Things to Do:*

TODAY—Fax article to clients

TODAY—Summarize meeting

March 13—Dr. Shipley's proposal

March 14—Office meeting and presentation

April 9—Gather information and send to seminar members

*Places to Go:*

1—Cleaners

2—Post office

3—Pick up film for attorney's brochure

4—Drop off basket to Jon's client

When you've completed a task, make a plus sign from the dash that precedes each task. This will keep your list organized and neat, and it is faster than scratching things out. To find unfinished tasks, you need only look for the dash.

At this point, ask yourself again whether it is absolutely necessary to do the task now. If you can keep these "parts" of your day in perspective, you can begin to get closer to what you want from life.

Think of these incremental tasks as vehicles to get you where you want to go—not as destinations in themselves. Nothing worth achieving is ever done quickly.

Enjoy the activities on the way to achieving your goals, just as you would enjoy the sights and tastes on the way to your vacation spot. Once you've reached your destination, you can decide on a new vacation spot for next year—in other words, one goal will follow another. Enjoy the sights!

## STAYING FLEXIBLE

To stay mentally flexible, don't push it! Even if you don't finish tasks as soon as you like, don't strain. "I make the most mistakes when I feel pinched for time," says Sarah, a medical transcriber. "The doctors I work for would rather have the files a day later than have mistakes. The only time that doesn't work is when they must be in court. I realized that's only 5% of the medical cases. I used to push hard 95% of the time and make many errors. I now work on court cases first, leaving everything else until later. What a difference it makes."

Also, remember that it's OK to change directions midway through a project. "Every year collecting all the information I need to give my accountant for taxes is excruciating. It's like pulling teeth," says Jane. "I'll do as much as my patience endures, and then I go do another job for a while. It helps keep me from going nuts."

A classic tip for maintaining mental flexibility is going for a walk to clear your head. "My best ideas come when I'm by myself and walking around the neighborhood," says Janet. "Ideas just come. Often, new ways of dealing with an old problem pop up."

By staying flexible, you can avoid being frozen by the enormity of a crisis or challenge. Janet, currently a director of business services for a school district, faced a big challenge when she decided to go back to school to get her bachelor's degree. Her husband, a law enforcement officer, had variable hours. "My life could not revolve around my husband. If it did, I'd have a great excuse not to go back to school." Janet has two children. What looked like an insurmountable task on the surface turned out to be a lesson in flexibility. "My seven-year-old daughter, fourteen-year-old son, and I would have dinner in the college dining commons, or I would bring a sandwich from home and we would have dinner on the grass outside my class. My son would spend the evening in the library where they had audio equipment, and do his homework. My seven-year-old would sometimes go with her brother or would come to class with me. Many nights my daughter slept in my arms while I listened and took class notes. We would get home around 9 P.M. We'd take baths, pick up some clutter . . . I made a choice between being a good student and having a clean house . . . clothes were on the sofa ready to be folded. Bedtime was 10 P.M.

"I had to give up sleep in order to do what I needed to do. I trained myself to wake up at 3 A.M. and study until 5, when I started to get ready for work and woke the children for school."

Janet now has her master's degree in education counseling and personnel services. Asked how she kept going, she muses, "I had to learn flexibility and not let the little things get in my way. I believe I had a force surrounding me that would protect me—I *owned* it. Getting my degree was worth the effort. I needed to do it. I believe education provides choices for me. . . . Without choices, I have nothing. . . . I had a good stable, secure job before, but I still needed to do this."

Janet confides that "there are women out there who are afraid to achieve. I have seen what happens to women who don't go after what they want, who can't be flexible with their time and their life. I told myself 'I'll never let that happen to me.' I've seen the bitterness and stagnation . . . caused mostly because they won't flow with what's happening to them at the time."

## IMPORTANT POINTS TO REMEMBER

Life brings crises and challenges. The way you *respond* to them determines the quality of your days and the quality of your life. Crisis and challenge bring opportunity.

When deciding what tasks or errands need to be done, you must stay flexible and look at the whole. Enjoy the process of getting where you want to go in life.

Decide what is absolutely necessary to do *now*. When a situation occurs that you *perceive* as a crisis, use reality checks to gain perspective.

# 10

# HOME SWEET HOME, INC. (THE PROS AND CONS OF WORKING AT HOME)

---

**K**nock-knock!

"Who's there?"

It doesn't matter. If you work at home, any interruption is a time-killer. Time management presents special challenges for the woman with a home office. Neighborhood mothers cheerfully volunteer your services (you are home, after all), friends assume that your "flexible" hours justify phone calls and visits during your work day, and the pile of dishes in the sink is screaming "Wash me!"

With a few home-office–management principles, you can put in a productive work day in far fewer hours than the traditional business timetable requires. You can learn to block out the endless list of interruptions and distractions that can—and usually do—occur on the home front.

---

## THE EIGHT BIGGEST TIME-WASTERS IN THE HOME OFFICE

When asked to list the top eight home-office time-busters,

**127**

the working women I surveyed responded with this list, which cites items in order of most distraction:

1. The need to clean the house
2. The telephone or visitors
3. The need to do the wash or ironing
4. Eating
5. The lack of information
6. The feeling of isolation
7. The need to run errands
8. The need to dress to see a client

Let's look at each one of these time-wasters and discuss how other working women handle them. Take bits and pieces from each idea to develop your own way of handling these problems. As in everything in this book, you need to pick and choose what works best with you.

## The Need to Clean the House

Before they can start working in their home offices, working women feel they *need* to have a clean house. The Traditional Homemaker feels that her work comes second. Therefore, the house must be clean before she can start on "her" work: a home job, paying the bills, her hobby, and so forth.

The Transitional Woman working at home also feels the need to have a clean and organized home. She views her income as supplemental; her real job is home and family. The fact that the Transitional Woman actually enjoys her work, in most cases, plays a secondary role.

The Achieving Woman who works at a home office can't wait to get started. But, being a perfectionist at heart, the need to have a clean and organized house is in the back of her mind, even though she may be able to ignore it.

Susan McKee, a public relations specialist, said: "I decided that my home would be both neat and clean. I realized, of course, that as a full-time professional there was not enough time to accomplish both. So I decided to keep my home neat myself while working harder to earn enough money to hire someone else to keep it clean."

Working women often perceive a clean home and a neat home in different ways. Jenny, a home-office working woman, says: "A clean home is spotless—bathroom sinks and mirrors shiny, all ironing up-to-date. A neat home is basically where things are picked up off the floor; beds are kinda made; dishes are neatly stacked in the sink; and dirty clothes are placed in different piles, ready to be washed."

### A HOUSE HELPER: A GREAT INVENTION

Most working women interviewed prefer a clean home, but accept a neat one. The Traditional Homemaker and Transitional Woman often think about having a house cleaner come in once or twice a month, but only a few follow through and hire one. The Achieving Woman usually hires someone to help clean the house once a week. She does the chores on the other days.

I want to suggest ways for you to have a house helper, no matter how much you make. A house helper can be a neighbor you trade off with once a week or once a month; a teenager you pay minimum wage; an older child; an aunt; and/or, in some cases, a full-fledged housekeeper.

Tina, a Traditional Homemaker, works 20 hours a week. When she works, she has a hard time keeping up with just the basic cleaning. Tina found, however, that her next-door neighbor didn't mind cleaning—what her neighbor hated was grocery shopping. The result was a beneficial trade-off for both of them. Tina shops for both families on Saturday, and her neighbor cleans Tina's house three hours a week. This works out fine for both of them.

I have a friend who hires a janitorial service three times a year to clean house and wash windows. There are, however, other ways to solve this problem.

## BEDROOM PLUS ONE

Cindy, a home-office mom, makes her three children responsible for their bedrooms plus one other room. These rooms need to be neat. If not, the children can't play outside, watch television, or talk on the phone. "They're responsible for whatever needs to be done in their rooms. For example, nine-year-old Claire has to keep his room neat, but this month takes care of the smaller bathroom, too. He washes the sink basin and cleans the mirror daily. He also makes sure there are neatly folded clean towels on the rack." When asked if this helps get Cindy prepared to work in her office, she quickly states, "I couldn't do it otherwise. There's only one of me. Why not use every member of the household?"

## THIRTY MINUTES IN THE MORNING

Gail, a realtor, straightens her house in the morning before she starts making phone calls in her home office. "I give myself 30 minutes to pick up whatever needs to be done. I take another break at noon if I'm home and wash the dishes in the sink from the night before. It doesn't take time out of my work day, and it's a good break."

# Telephone Calls and Visitors

If you're going to do business from home, you need to honestly treat your work as a business. It's difficult for others to treat you seriously and professionally if you do not honestly perceive yourself as serious and professional.

The telephone is one of your most important business tools. In fact, the telephone forms the basic line of communication between you and your client, and between you and more business information. As in any other type of communication, the working woman must handle it with care. Professional communication is critical to a good relationship with clients, vendors, and employees.

When you are a professional who works at home, projecting a professional image may also be important when dealing with friends and family. You may have to let them know, gently but firmly, that the fact that you are home does not mean that you are available. Let family and friends know what your business hours are. If they interrupt you during those times, suggest they call or come back later. Realize that you play a role in determining the productivity of your work time by deciding when you answer the phone or door, how you screen your calls, and who you give your phone numbers to.

## A SECOND LINE, PLEASE

It is vital to have a business phone with its own phone number. Because many working women want to keep their operating costs to a minimum, they tend to use the home phone for business. After all, goes the thinking, "I can't afford a second line," or "I don't really need it." Wrong!

There's nothing more unprofessional than when your client calls you at your home office and your child answers the phone or your answering machine takes the call with a cute message left by you, your husband, or your children.

## TO ANSWER OR NOT TO ANSWER

Sue, a writer, does not give out her phone number. "I found, even after I published my first two books, people called to chat, since I was at home. I never had a second line put in, because I rarely use this phone. I found that if I did not give out my phone number, except in rare situations, I had control of who I wanted to speak to."

Sue takes control of her work time by not answering calls when she needs to concentrate. "Every time I was on a roll, the telephone would ring, and when I first started writing I felt I had to answer it 'just in case.' Now, I don't even notice when it rings."

I asked Sue if she used an answering machine.

"No, because I can still hear who it is and then I may want to talk to them. The people I do business with and my good friends know not to call me between 10 A.M. and 7 P.M. My long-distance friends and I write to each other."

Sharon finds that her secretarial business depends on the telephone. "I have an active social life and felt that I needed to get my own business phone. This way I know how to answer the phone, a social 'Hi,' or a business 'Sharon here.' I also found the second phone made me feel professional. I don't know if this is a consequence or not, but my secretarial business started improving right about the time I invested in another phone line."

Gail, the realtor, finds that the phone is her most precious business asset. "I could save a lot of money by using an answering machine, but I'm in the 'people' business. I personally don't like answering machines . . . in fact, you can almost always tell when someone is leaving a message on a machine, rather than talking to a real person on the other side of the phone.

"I invested in a 24-hour answering service to receive my calls. When I am at my home office and I don't want to be disturbed, I let the answering service pick up the call. This is a good way to check on their service—how many rings before they pick up the receiver. I leave instructions with the answering service when I'm working on special projects. I could never do that with my answering machine."

Another reason working women invest in an answering service is to keep their operating costs down without hiring a full-time secretary. Cindy says, "Most of my clients think I have a secretary . . . it sounds professional. There's a lot of competition out there . . . everyone and their sister-in-law seems to be in real estate now. If I can be a little different and more personable and professional while I'm at it, why not?"

## The Need to Do Wash

What do you do with the piles of wash on the floor in the laundry room after you've taken the time to sort through them? What about the comments from the family: "Where's my shirt, my thermal underwear, my P.E. shirt, my sweats?" After all, you *are* home and "should" be able to get a simple task like the wash done, especially if the garment doesn't need to be ironed. What do you *do* with your time anyway, working woman? If this is echoed in your home or within your mind, stop! It's important to let other family members know that you are not a laundry. Here are some ideas to redistribute the burden of laundry.

### ONE-DAY SERVICE

Impossible? Not if you have a well-developed system. You can devise a system whereby wash becomes a family event. Cindy developed an "overnight" area in the laundry room. It is the responsibility of each family member to put the clothes he or she needs the next day in that spot. If he or she forgets to put it in the laundry room before 5 P.M. the evening before it's needed, S-O-R-R-Y.

"It helps me figure out what wash is a priority for the family. This way I don't have to yell and scream and ask for their clothes or have them whine at me in the morning for whatever it is that they need. . . . Our mornings go so much more smoothly now," says Cindy.

### WASH IT AND DUMP IT

Both Cindy and Gail put in a load of wash first thing in the morning, before going to their home offices. "I get at least four loads in a day. The first one I do first thing in the morning. At lunchtime I put the wet wash in the dryer and put a new load in the washer. Then I take an afternoon break, and repeat the cycle again after dinner. I take equal piles to the children's bedrooms. The kids are then responsible for folding, putting the clothes away, and putting the ironables back in the laundry room. . . . It's a great system as long as I don't go into the children's bedrooms after I dump the clean clothes there."

## The Urge to Nosh

It is common for working women to nosh themselves into oblivion during their working hours at their home offices. It is a natural inclination to go to the refrigerator or pantry when they're home. This is especially true when they want to take a break or are procrastinating in starting on a project.

### FRUIT, VEGETABLES, AND GUM

Marty is a pharmaceutical representative and keeps her office at home. She finds she has no problem with noshing on her "out" days, when she keeps appointments with doctors. But the days she stays at her office at home, she gets a bad case of the noshies. "I started by eating everything I could find in the pantry—handfuls of cereal, cookies, and chips. At the end of the day I felt awful, I was so stuffed, but I hadn't eaten anything nutritionally sound. I now buy loads of sugarless gum."

After going through the nosh stage, women start to gain pounds and inches where there weren't any before. Before Marty started chewing gum, she tried getting into three dressy outfits one weekend. *"None* of them fit. I was horrified. . . . I couldn't get the skirts over my hips . . . and I'm not fat."

Ethel, an interior designer, went through the eating stage and gained weight. She decided to do something about it. "The more I read and experienced how I felt when I ate healthy, the more I got into nutrition. My husband calls me a health nut, but I tell him I'm just a healthy eater."

I asked Ethel how she keeps her weight down and avoids the eating binge. She says she has a bag of raisins or an assortment of dry, low-sugar cereals at her drafting table. "When I'm thinking, I just absentmindedly grab for the cereal or raisins. That does the trick. The by-product is that it makes me thirsty, so I drink a lot more water now than I ever did before. I have bottled water sent to my house. Most of my breaks are to go to the bathroom."

Katherine, a reading tutor, has a routine that works for her. "I go to the gym three times a week, in the morning, and work out and lift weights for about 1½ hours each time. I come home, take a shower, get dressed, put on makeup, and work the rest of the day. I also buy diet soft drinks by the case. I'm really conscious of my weight, so I only keep healthy things in the refrigerator. I usually eat a tuna-fish sandwich for lunch. It works for me."

Shelly, a consultant who works out of her home office, loves to eat and has a lot of energy. "I could live on fresh fruit and vegetables. I love grapes, so I often have them on my desk. It's better for you than smoking, and I find I pop one in when I'm thinking about things. . . . I've skinned them with my teeth, I've rolled them around in my mouth, and I've sucked on them more than once or twice.

"If I'm not too tired the night before, I cut up carrots or pineapple to eat the following day. I have little packages of fresh fruit and vegetables all over in my refrigerator. I munch on dried fruit also, but I don't open the package of the dried fruit unless I don't have anything in the refrigerator."

## The Lack of Information

It is a rare home office that has a complete library of
resource books, and many working women feel that they
cannot do a good job without them. Few working women
have the time and money to develop a large library. What
do you do?

### LIBRARY AS OFFICE

The library can be a very good office away from home.
Resource books are nearby, dozens of newspapers and
magazine articles are within reach, and you're away from
the telephone and refrigerator. For Linda, a freelance
copyeditor, the library is her permanent office. "It's rent-
free. The money I save pays for supplies. Research items
are available and close at hand. I'm away from my office
phone but close to a public phone, should I need to get
in touch with a client."

Many libraries provide all the essential equipment:
typewriter, computer, pay phone, resource material, people to speak to, and peace and quiet away from familiar
sounds.

## The Feeling of Isolation

Working at a home office is lonely. There's no one to talk
to, get you motivated, or to exchange ideas. Breaks usually consist of noshing, cleaning, or telephone interruptions.
For weeks at a time, one is a very lonely number.

### TAKE STEPS TO LESSEN LONELINESS

To decrease loneliness:

- Start your day at a coffee shop two or three times
  a week. Bring some work you need to do, read the
  local paper, or plan your daily tasks. Surrounding

yourself with people early in the day has a tendency to motivate you.

- During a break, call a friend to say hi. Keep the conversation under 10 minutes. Calling friends at your convenience is a great way to stay in touch.
- Eat lunch *away* from your desk. Go to the park, another room, or treat yourself to a lunch date. If you worked outside your home, you'd most likely eat out.

### DEVELOP A NETWORK

Having a home office requires that you stay in touch with your competition and others in your business, locally as well as nationally. It also requires that you share important information and make good decisions. What happens if there is only a staff of one—you?

To be effective in business as well as fight the debilitating sense of isolation common to those who work alone, you must develop a network. Here are some tips about getting plugged in:

- Put together a group of people in your profession or a group of other home-office workers.
- Faithfully attend state or national association conferences.
- Join and regularly attend Chamber of Commerce meetings.
- Stay abreast of community events; add your expertise in a volunteer role.
- Plan two lunches or breakfasts a week with people you enjoy and with whom you can be yourself and feel safe to share concerns and doubts.
- Write a press release to your local newspaper twice a year, just to let others know you're still out there.

## The Need to Run Errands

Since the major responsibility for significant others usually rests with the working woman, she is endlessly running errands. She does everything from picking up her daughter's ballet or soccer shoes, wax for the children's new braces, milk for breakfast, and cards for sick friends or clients.

To decrease the time you spend away from your desk, take inventory, stockpile, offload, and anticipate.

### TAKE INVENTORY OF YOUR MOST COMMON ERRANDS

On errands, where do you find yourself the most? In the dairy, produce, or bathroom department of a grocery store; the card or cold-remedy department of a drugstore; the gift area in a department store; or the library, checking out encyclopedias? After you have an idea where you spend most of your time on errands, you can take action and save a lot of time.

If you frequently find yourself in the places mentioned in the list that follows, take the recommended action.

- **Dairy department:** Have delivered to your door your milk, eggs, orange juice, and any other items you often run out of. The increase in cost is only pennies when you compare the gas, time, and time-pressure taken off you. In fact, in most cases, delivery is far cheaper if all this is taken into account.

- **Produce department:** If you have a family that enjoys fresh produce, then buy fruit and vegetables with longlasting appeal. Buy green bananas, cranberries, apples, dates, figs, cauliflower, broccoli, carrots, celery, and zucchini, to name a few.

- **Card stores:** Taking the time to send cards is not only thoughtful, it can be beneficial. I will more readily take the time to do something for someone who has, by sending a card, been thoughtful or appreciative.

One way to decrease the number of trips to the card store is to start your own card collection, with major emphasis in areas that are prominent in your life. Your card selections probably relate to your life stage. Are a lot of your friends getting married, having babies, getting divorced, changing careers, getting promoted, getting sick, or traveling? Remembering these occasions helps you nurture your support system at work, at home, and personally. Taking the time to nurture your networking system saves you time and energy when that support is necessary.

To keep track of birthdays and anniversaries, keep a calendar separate from your daily calendar. Since these dates come up year after year, get a date book without day or year, only month and date. You can easily make one up:

      June 1     Casey Richards
          2
          3

If you have a supply of cards on hand, you can simply go to your card drawer instead of the store. This method not only saves time, but your date book will help you remember important events year after year. Your friends, clients, and family will be impressed.

- **Cold-remedy department:** If you find yourself in the cold-remedy department, keep a few extra bottles of Tylenol or Aspergum in your medicine chest. I would suggest you keep vitamin C on hand also, in the form of tablets or fresh oranges.
- **Gift stores:** Buy gifts when they're on sale. With your date book at your side, you can save time and money in choosing the right gift. The working woman often has to settle for what is left because she didn't have the time to go shopping beforehand. Plus, the gift is more expensive because it is

a last-ditch effort to get something. P.S.: Keep the gift wrap near the gift closet.

- **Library:** If your child has started doing reports and term papers, maybe it's time to check into buying a set of encyclopedias. If the cost is prohibitive, set up a neighbor check-out system with a family that has a set. If this idea proves too difficult, you can always make a trip to the library twice a month.

The last idea requires an understanding of what projects will be due in your child's class in the next two weeks. It's a good way to keep informed of your children's projects, keep an eye on their homework, and follow up.

## The Need to Dress to See a Client

What happens when you're pounding on the computer, getting your work taken care of, and a client needs to see you immediately? You don't sound very pleased over the phone, because you weren't planning to see any clients today; you're in a bathrobe and you have oily, unmanageable hair. Your client, on the other side of the receiver, can't see you (thank God) and perceives your unwillingness to visit as "something must be wrong." Here are some alternatives.

### WAKE UP AND WORK IT

It is important for the home-based working woman to wake up, take a shower, and get ready for work. In other words, put on your makeup, make sure your hair is the way you like it (even spritz it if you want), and get dressed in your working attire. This serves three important functions. First, you feel as if you're at work; therefore, you perform at a higher capacity. Second, at a moment's notice, you're able to visit a client or pick up something at the printer's or anywhere else. Third, getting dressed and looking good increases your self-esteem. It's a lot easier to think you're ugly, fat, or undesirable when you see yourself in a bathrobe or sweats and with messy hair most days.

## IMPORTANT POINTS TO REMEMBER

Working from a home office presents special challenges. The eight most common time interruptions are the need to clean the house, the telephone or visitors, the need to do the wash or ironing, eating, not having enough resource material, feeling isolated, the need to run errands, and the need to dress to see a client.

When the need to clean hits, remember that it's OK to have a neat, rather than a clean, house. The telephone is your friend as long as you are in control of incoming calls. Limit in-person visits, too. Turn the need to wash into a family affair. Go ahead and nosh—just make sure you eat fruit and vegetables. Use the library as your office on days you need resource information. To offset the feeling of isolation, eat breakfast out, take outside breaks, and develop a network of friends and business associates.

Take inventory of your most common errands. Stockpile what you need and find other ways to reduce trips. Dress professionally every day you work.

Treat yourself seriously, and others will too. Your attitude shows your clients and suppliers that you are professional and available for them.

# 11

# MIRROR, MIRROR ON THE DESK: ORGANIZING YOUR DESK TO REFLECT PRIORITIES

---

The myth about the correlation between Mensa minds and disaster-zone desks is best left to cartoonists and dilettantes. The cold reality is that women who juggle jobs, kids, and husbands or lovers can't afford to spend precious minutes hunting for a buried memo or a misplaced love letter.

Whether at home or at the office, the condition of your working space reflects your level of professionalism and ultimately has an impact on all areas of your performance.

Clearing your desk is the first step to maintaining a business space that will help you work efficiently.

## CLEARING YOUR DESK—AND KEEPING IT CLEAR

As a rule, you may have an organized desk. But every two or three weeks you get busy. Papers pile on your desk, and then you have a messy desk.

I suggest to my clients that they take their unfiled papers and stack them neatly under their desks. When papers come through the fax or into your in-box, simply stack them on top of the others down there. This keeps your desk clear for the entire time it takes you to complete your task. If you have 20 minutes between appointments, then take the stack on the floor and file the papers in the correct spots.

No matter where you keep the papers, however, the key is to organize them in a way that's meaningful to you. Audrey, a schoolteacher, says: "I have so many papers to read through each day. I started two stacks of papers on my desk. One is for papers to grade, and the other is for memos. My goal is to work through at least half of each stack each day. I'm able to keep up this way."

Elaine, a secretary to four people, keeps one large stack on her desk. The papers are in order by immediacy of completion. "I keep the stack on the right side of my desk. When realtors come in to give me more work, they see how far I've progressed. It's stopped a lot of 'I need this immediately.' I only hear that when they really mean it. Otherwise, their material goes under the stack and the size of the stack lets them know when they'll get it."

Kim works at a printing business. "I keep two lists on my desk now. One is for rush jobs and the other is for normal turnaround. We get people all the time that say they need something yesterday. Everything we did had to be done immediately. I couldn't find anything on my desk. We started charging $15 for rush orders. We found that over 80% of the people don't really need the printing done ASAP. For the 20% of people that really do need it immediately, they gladly pay the extra $15. I now have an orderly desk and happier customers."

## Organize the Top of the Desk

Important things go on top of your desk and stay there: a paperweight, paper-clip holder with clips inside, stapler, pencil-and-pen holder, small clock, telephone, fax machine, and one or two small *chatzkies* (knickknacks). Everything else goes somewhere else, including the pictures.

Pictures are wonderful and they make us feel good, but they distract us from our work. Family relationships are never routine. They are either on a high or on a low. If you glance at the picture during either peak, it will tend to take your mind away from your immediate task.

Your computer needs to have its own table. Otherwise, your entire desk is taken up with this machine and you cannot see your work.

I define the word *clearance* as the ability to see a neat desk when you enter and leave your office. Clearance provides a huge feeling of satisfaction, completion, and organization. Clearance gives way to open, creative thinking.

One technique for achieving clearance is what I call the three-*D*'s filing system. The system uses three manila files, which are kept on top of the desk.

### THE THREE-*D*'S FILING SYSTEM

Each *D* in the three-*D*'s filing system stands for the time I must do something.

- Do it this morning.
- Do it this afternoon.
- Do it now.

I assign a file folder to each deadline, and I file papers related to each deadline in the appropriate folder.

The "do it this morning" stack needs to be done before lunch. In most cases, these papers need a signature, a quick review for errors, or a yes or no response. This work needs to be completed in the morning so that others can continue the process.

The "do it this afternoon" pile needs to be done after lunch. Again, in most cases, the work requires a small amount of time and energy. But, because it requires so little time, the tendency is to put these tasks off and the process of procrastination begins. Procrastination begets procrastination—and frustration for others.

The "do it now" papers need to be done as soon as I receive them. This stack can be kept small by keeping up with the first two *D*'s. Much in the "do it now" file relates to "putting out fires" resulting from delays or procrastination.

Now that the top of the desk is clear, turn your attention to the desk drawers.

## Organize the Desk Drawers

Make sure your desk has at least three drawers: a center drawer and two side drawers. Turn each drawer into an organized filing area.

**The Center Drawer**   In the center drawer, store extra pencils and pens, ruler, stamps, and phone directories from organizations, your children's classrooms, and such. Keep a telephone file in this drawer for easy access. I use labeled manila folders to organize my papers.

**The Side Drawers**   Use one side drawer to store stationery, envelopes, scissors, extra change, makeup, Kleenex, and legal pads.

Use the bottom side drawer for active files. These are the files that you constantly work with. By putting them back in the same place every time, you will alleviate the need to search for them. If you find what you need quickly, you keep yourself from becoming distracted by nonessential tasks.

## Use the Area Under the Desk

You can use the space under your desk for more than overflow from your desk top. Under my desk, I stack the mail that needs to go home. I keep my purse there as well as anything else that needs to go home from the office. It helps me remember to take things home.

In addition, I keep the telephone, my to-do list, and my errand list under my desk. This serves two functions. First, I must constantly bend down, which promotes circulation to my upper body. Second, what I need to see is easily accessible without my having to open, shut, and bump the desk drawers. (I found that, when I constantly opened the drawers, I got runs in my hose.)

In addition, I keep a 50.7-ounce water container under my desk. Besides being out of the way, it is unlikely to spill on papers, and its location keeps me bending.

I suggest that you do *not* have a trash basket under your desk or anywhere in your office. If you like to eat fruit in your office, having the trash can nearby is asking for an office with the odor of banana peels and apple cores.

I simply throw my trash on the ground in one not-so-neat pile. When my mind wanders, I get up and throw it away *outside* my office. Sitting in one position for several hours takes its toll on the working woman's back, shoulders, wrists, and legs. The process of throwing the papers down, bending down to get them, and walking into another area gets the circulation moving.

Some days when I'm particularly antsy, I try to throw the trash into the can while taking a break in the kitchen area. I give myself two points for every "basket" I make. I've met some nice office neighbors this way. In fact, I met a client by doing this. I threw several baskets one day, and the event got me talking with a man who was waiting to see his accountant. Next thing I knew, we were exchanging cards. Two months later he became a marketing client. Moral: Some baskets are worth more points than others!

Now that you have developed a few habits that have transformed your desk into a model of organization, develop one more habit that will get each new day off to a good start.

*Get Set for Tomorrow*

Clear your desk before leaving your office each day. Then
place in the middle of the desk whatever you must deal
with first tomorrow. This will help you focus on what needs
to be done as soon as you enter your office.

Focus is important for working women. Because we
play so many roles, our minds can easily wander away from
the task at hand. Anything that disrupts focus is what I
call mind interference. By placing your priority task in
the middle of your desk, you can avoid mind interference,
quickly don your professional persona, and get to work.

## ESTABLISHING A "BACK ROOM"

You don't necessarily need a back room, but you do need
an area that is away from your desk. This "back room"
area will help keep your main work space organized and
allow you to be productive. Keep dormant files, research
articles, press releases, old projects, and other inactive but
important papers in the back room. The copy machine
also goes there.

You can establish a back room, even if your work space
doesn't have one. If you don't have walls dividing the two
areas, use furniture. Use a bookshelf, use a couch, or use
large plants to surround the back room area. The most
important element is that you should not be able to see
the inactive files. You need to alleviate mind interference.

*Use Bookcases for Filing*

Bookcases are great for filing books, magazines, articles,
or newsletters. Put articles and newsletters in labeled
manila folders and file them by topic. Sarah, a Transitional

Woman, says: "I do a lot of reading. I keep magazines and make copies of special articles I think I'll need in my work, in my relationships, or when I want to decide on places I want to visit eventually. I've started a good library of information."

As you find articles or addresses you want to keep, put a yellow stickum note on the proper page and write the purpose of keeping the article. This saves time; you need not leaf through the magazine, book, or article to find the information you want or why you wanted to keep it in the first place. Make directions simple: "Make a copy and file under Administration," "Make a copy and send to Janet," or "Write for more information."

## DOING A WEEKLY CLEANUP

Weekly cleanups are a must. No matter what system you use, there are times when you don't have time to file your material in its proper place. Again, simply stack the papers, folders, ads, and other material in a neat pile. The best time to file this stack is in the afternoon, if you're a morning person, or in the morning, if you're an afternoon person. Two things to remember: Do not file Monday mornings, because filing will slow you down for the day, and do not file Friday afternoons, because you won't get it done—you'll be thinking of the weekend and you'll be tired. Other than that, go at it!

## KEEPING YOURSELF FROM OVERDOING IT

So far, you have organized your desk and created a work space to maximize your efficiency. Don't get carried away in your desire for clearance, however. The only times when

your desk should be completely clear are on your first and
last days of work. Other than these times, always keep these
three things on your desk:

- Your reference point
- The active project
- A timepiece

A reference point is an object that gives you a feeling
of security. It establishes for you a familiar environment
in which you can feel free to create, develop, and work.
If you have more than one reference point, that's fine—
just don't use photos of family or friends.

Ann's reference point, or personal *chatzky*, was a crystal
unicorn. "The janitor moved it once, and I had the worst
day. I like it right by the phone, where I can see it clearly.
I know that sounds superstitious, but I can't help it."

The active project should be on your desk at all times.
If you have three major projects to complete, place two
to the side or under your desk. And, as mentioned earlier
in this chapter, put the active file in the middle of your
desk when you leave for the evening.

You must know the time to keep appointments, follow
progress, and give your mind and body a break for lunch.
Therefore, always keep a timepiece on your desk. If you
have unlimited time for a project, turn it away from you
if you want. If not, have it face you.

## IMPORTANT POINTS TO REMEMBER

Maintaining an organized desk and file system is vital to
getting work done efficiently. Use your desk as your filing system—each drawer has important functions. The
area under your desk can play an organizational role as
well.

Weekly cleanups are essential for keeping your office neat and papers placed properly. Don't clear your desk completely, however. Keep on your desk objects that impart security, task focus, and time awareness.

Be creative. Develop a desk and filing system that works for you. Be sure the system provides efficiency, exercise, stability, and focus.

# 12

# I Think It's a Definite Maybe (A Quick Guide to Decision Making)

The decisions a working woman makes sometimes seem to have magnified importance because of the many roles she plays. For example, a decision she makes at work can affect workers up and down the hierarchy; in addition, because she is probably the family member who coordinates care for the children and home, the same decision can have an almost immediate effect on her family. Her personal time is affected as well, and the whole interplay of work, family, and self must find a new equilibrium. Working women realize how important their decisions are, and to them the need to make decisions often seems like an extra-heavy burden.

As women, we tend to have two problems with decision making. The first concerns the decisions themselves. We tend to choose what is safe; in other words, our decisions tend to support the status quo. This chapter will discuss how, in resisting change in decision making, we

**153**

are sometimes wasting time and cheating ourselves. The second common decision-making problem for women is indecision. Whether disguised as procrastination, reconsideration, or what economist Pareto calls "the paralysis of analysis," indecision is a habit worth conquering. By studying your own decision-making patterns, you can become decisive; this chapter will show you how.

## RESISTING THE URGE TO RESIST CHANGE

Most working women do not like change. The Traditional Homemaker likes her life just the way it is. Routine habits and patterns give her a sense of security. She feels that, if she rocks the boat, someone in the family will be adversely affected. You often hear the Traditional Homemaker say, "I'll go back to work [school] when my children are in school"; "I can't go to dance lessons—they're at night, and I don't want to leave my husband home alone"; "I'll spend more time on me when the kids have left the house—I have all my life"; and "I'll start traveling when my husband retires."

Ann, who travels half the year with her semiretired husband, says: "I stayed home and raised three children. I would only plan to do things during the day while my husband and children were gone. I kept a tiny room in the house to do my artwork. If only I knew then what I know now. I would have made the decision to rent a studio and work on my art every day."

Like the Traditional Homemaker, the Transitional Woman usually tries to put off anything that sounds like change. She says she's too busy for it: "I don't have time to do anything but raise my kids and work. I couldn't add one more appointment, meeting, or obligation to my schedule if my life depended on it."

Susan, a controller for a medium-sized business, says: "I was so locked into my schedule, that my car could have made trips without me. I had set times for everything and wouldn't even consider any change."

The Achieving Woman doesn't mind changing the status quo of managing her work and priorities, providing she does not need to take time to relearn anything. She knows she can get more done if she stays with the tried-and-true methods. But are the old methods necessarily the best?

Change brings risk, it's true. But change also brings newness, freshness, and a different perspective. Great things can come of change; intellectually, most of us know this. Emotionally, however, we fight change and may not accept it unless we are forced to.

Susan, the Transitional Woman and controller, was forced to make changes when she was diagnosed with multiple sclerosis (MS). "Everything changed," she says. "I came home during lunch to rest. I put the children in an afternoon center where they learned how to work with computers, my husband and children washed the dishes every night, and we hired a cleaning lady twice a month—something I had wanted to do for years. I don't know why it took something drastic to help my life change for the better, but it did."

Shirley had always had trouble with overcommitting herself. She couldn't say no to anyone. "I didn't want anyone to be upset with me. I placed incredible expectations on myself. Sometimes I was so tired I couldn't fall asleep for hours." Shirley's life changed when she was laid off at work. "I started my own business, which I had wanted to do for years. Unless the activity dealt with my business or the kids' welfare, I said no. For the first time in my adult life, I am doing things because I want to rather than because I think I should. Once I practiced a few no's, it wasn't so hard to do. Making those decisions helped me create more time for the two areas that were most important to me at the time: my children and my business."

The moral of these stories is that you must embrace change. Eventually, change may well embrace you, so why not do it on your own terms? The sooner you make a change, the sooner you will enjoy the benefits of change, which often include a new outlook and enthusiasm for life. Developing the ability to change means developing the ability to take control of your life.

## Tips for Developing a Change-Receptive Personality

Cultivating a positive attitude toward change takes work in all areas of your life. It involves doing things that make you feel less secure and self-confident and exposing yourself to new perspectives and information. The following tips outline some helpful activities that will help you grow into a woman who can not only take change in stride, but initiate it.

- Analyze your Personal Motivational Lifestyle. If the way you are using your time is out of synch with your priorities, you are probably under too much stress to accept change. Shift your time use so it matches your priorities. The burden of stress should lessen, and you will be more resilient.

- Make a goal and reward yourself when you achieve it. Achieving a goal will make you realize your power, and this will increase your belief that you can handle any change that comes along.

- Discuss fears and concerns with a trustworthy friend, a member of the clergy, or a therapist. Fears and concerns don't seem as extreme when they're out in the open. You may realize that you have more capacity to deal with all aspects of life—including change—than you thought you did.

- Try new scheduling ideas. The simple fact of doing

things in a different order or in a new place can help you exercise your flexibility. If you usually go to the gym in the morning, for example, try going in the evening. You might not like it at first, but try it for one month. A long trial period will tell you if the new arrangement has any unexpected benefits. On the job, try changing meeting times around. If you usually meet at breakfast, see how meeting at a different time works. Don't fall into the trap of saying "I can't. There's no other time that will work."

- Bring in new people. To stay open to different perspectives, talk to as many different people as you can. Surround yourself with people who have fresh ideas. This might include appointing or serving on a task force so that you can expose yourself to as many different perspectives as is practical.

Once you have seen the benefits of staying open to change, I doubt you will ever want to be any other way. Many women are stuck, however. They cannot accept or make changes because they cannot make decisions. The remainder of this chapter will discuss the psychological factors that drive decision making, and the discussion will include a section that will help you assess your own decision-making habits.

## UNDERSTANDING DECISION-MAKING PATTERNS

As you might expect, the emotional motivations in decision making coincide closely with the three Personal Motivational Lifestyles. Not all women—not even women with the same Personal Motivational Lifestyle—handle their emotions in the same way, however. As a result, there are several distinct patterns of decision making.

## Emotional Motivations

One of the primary motivators in decision making is fear. The type of fear that a woman must face bears a strong correlation to the type of woman she is.

One of the Traditional Homemaker's greatest fears is failure. She considers herself a personal failure if home and family needs are not met. Her basic premise is that she's here to provide all the necessary emotional support for her family.

In my experience, the Transitional Woman's greatest fear is success. If she spends an extended amount of time at work, she may not only get promoted, but she may have less time for her husband or children. Likewise, the single Transitional Woman does not want to get too involved with work, because she wants to be available for marriage, children, or travel.

The Achieving Woman's greatest fear is rejection, particularly in the workplace. Her fear of rejection from her work peers, clients, management, and boss drives her to overachieve. The Achieving Woman brings her need to overachieve to her relationships as well as her work. If she can't get perfection, then she perceives a problem and may opt to quit. Marriage and perfection do not go hand in hand; therefore, among the three types of women discussed in this book, Achieving Women have the highest percentage of divorces.

## Patterns of Decision Making

In my work with women, I have distinguished six types of decision makers:

- Analyzers
- Information overloaders
- Risk takers

- Traumatizers
- Fence sitters
- Procrastinators

Each of these types of women brings a distinct psycho-logical perspective to the decision-making process, and each type's decision-making style has an impact on the woman's time and the quality of the decision she makes.

In the sections that follow, try to see yourself. If you see that you are prey to the pitfalls of your decision-making style, make the changes that are recommended for your specific type.

### THE ANALYZER

This woman needs to look at *all* aspects of an issue. This is helpful, to a point. There comes a time, however, when further analysis wastes time and is counterproductive.

Psychological perspective: The analyzer is afraid to make a mistake because she thinks it will make her look dumb or foolish.

Time implication: Because the analyzer spends time reworking the same information, her decision-making style can waste time.

Positive action: Make a decision based on the infor-mation and your experience. If your decision could have been better, then accept that fact and correct the decision. We learn from our mistakes, but only true leaders accept and correct their errors with pride.

### THE INFORMATION OVERLOADER

The woman in this category keeps getting more and more information. She never makes it to the analysis stage, let alone the decision stage.

Psychological perspective: Being an expert is very important to this woman. She feels that, if she misses one new discovery or point, she will not be perceived as the expert. She will lose status and let her colleagues down.

Time implication: Because gathering new information takes priority over decision making, this decision-making style wastes time.

Positive action: Get information from no more than seven sources. I have found that seven sources is usually a sufficient number to allow me to spot trends. After reviewing the seven sources, make the decision!

### THE RISK TAKER

This woman makes decisions based on equal parts of information and her own gut feelings or experience. The risk taker feels that too much information is redundant and a waste of time. She feels she has the necessary arsenal to make the decision.

Psychological perspective: This woman is not afraid to take risks.

Time implication: This decision-making style wastes little time.

Positive action: If the decision is negative, change it!

### THE TRAUMATIZER

This woman makes a decision and then constantly worries about it. Making the decision is not time-consuming for these women, but the complaining and rehashing afterward sap energy as well as time.

Psychological perspective: She doubts her ability to make sound decisions.

Time implication: The traumatizer wastes time worrying when she could be accomplishing her goals.

Positive action: Keep a list of your major decisions and write down their outcomes. Were most outcomes positive or negative? Chances are good that most of your outcomes were positive. This will help you gain self-confidence in your decision-making ability.

## THE FENCE SITTER

This woman finds it excruciatingly difficult to make decisions. For every reason she finds to make one decision, she finds one that moves her to make the opposite decision. She cannot prioritize the reasons related to the decision. Her constant comment is, "On the other hand...."

Psychological perspective: The fear of making a mistake is this woman's predominant fear.

Time implication: This decision-making style is a major time-waster.

Positive action: Make a list of advantages and disadvantages. Rate each advantage or disadvantage from 1 to 10, according to its importance. The decision should become much clearer.

## THE PROCRASTINATOR

This woman waits to make decisions until "it's time." She says, "I'll make it eventually." The result is that she is forced to make a decision because time has run out, thereby lessening her feeling of responsibility. This woman rarely takes the initiative in life. She lets most things "just happen."

Psychological perspective: The procrastinator has a difficult time accepting responsibility and feels overwhelmed easily.

Time implication: The fact that the procrastinator waits until the last minute is in itself a time-waster. The procrastinator's decisions are likely to be so ill considered that further time is wasted in reworking and reimplementing them.

Positive action: Change your thinking. A forced choice is no choice.

---

## BEATING INDECISION

Once you realize that decisions don't have to be perfect, you will free yourself from the paralyzing anxiety that can

lead to indecision. In fact, the mistakes you make in decision making can be a source of strength for you as you
approach future decisions. To explain this, I often tell
women what Frank Sinatra said about painting:

> You see, the great thing about painting is that a
> lot of paintings don't work, and it dramatizes what
> happens in life. When you first start painting, and
> it doesn't work out, you're devastated. But you keep
> painting. Then you're not bothered by your mis-
> takes. You just say, "The next time will be better."
> That's what happens in life. That's why I wouldn't
> change anything: Because I made mistakes, but
> those mistakes taught me how to live.

## IMPORTANT POINTS TO REMEMBER

Women tend to have two problems with decision making.
First, we tend to make "safe" decisions, decisions that
minimize change. Second, we tend to be indecisive. To
make the most of our time and our lives, we must learn
to embrace change, which often brings vast benefits. By
understanding our decision-making patterns, we can con-
quer indecisiveness.

Decision making is often based on fear. As a rule, the
Traditional Homemaker fears failure, the Transitional
Woman fears success, and the Achieving Woman fears
rejection. These women, because of their fears, waste time
with indecision.

It's taken you years to "perfect" your personal decision-
making patterns. If you've made the decision to change
your style, just do it.

# 13

# THE WRITE STUFF

Even the best and brightest of us must sometimes admit that a short pencil is better than a long memory. Note taking and journal keeping are two invaluable tools for working women. To those who harbor an aversion to the written word: *Beware.*

As we evaluate our time-management skills, we often discover a surprising discrepancy between how we think we spend our time and how we actually fill our hours. A time log can quickly pinpoint wasted time and dispel the belief that "I don't have a spare minute!"

In this chapter, you will learn how to use starter sheets, time-log sheets, task sheets, and your calendar to discover what you need to do and how you are using your time, to organize your efforts, and to keep yourself motivated. You will also learn ways to use lists to make yourself more effective at work and at home.

## USING A STARTER SHEET

The mind is a fascinating computer. It's compact, portable, and has an exhaustive list of programs. For preventive maintenance of your "mental computer," you must write

down important thoughts, feelings, and ideas, and stay
positive. The starter sheet enables you to do all three.

To make a starter sheet, take a legal pad and write down
a paragraph, preferably a page, about what you want to
accomplish today and why it's important to do it today.
Separate this information into work, home, and personal
categories. This sheet serves two functions: It helps
organize your priorities in each area, and it prepares you
mentally for the day.

Analyze what you've written. This lets you think about
your day in an organized way. You may find that what you
thought was important to do today, is not. Or you may find
that writing your tasks down relieves stress, even though
you haven't done your tasks yet. The starter sheet helps
combine your conscious self with your unconscious self.
Writing ideas down gets you from the worry or procrastination mode into *action*.

Toni, a Transitional Woman, felt stressed. "My aunt
was coming to visit for the weekend. I had a project deadline coming up, several client events in the making, children out of school for spring break, and dinner to prepare
for ten the next night. And, thanks to Murphy's Law, my
cleaning lady had shown up two hours late.

"I wrote down what I thought needed doing. I also
noted my feelings. This relieved my stress. After I analyzed what I had written, here's what I decided to do. I
would work on my project while deep-conditioning my
hair, take a 20-minute walk, then wash my hair, let it dry
while working on three client files, take the children and
my aunt grocery shopping midafternoon, and start our
meal at 3:30 P.M.

"Somehow, it all worked. At 10:00 P.M. I fell asleep talking to my aunt, while sitting up!"

The next step, after preparing the one-page starter
sheet, is to transfer the important priorities for the day
onto your time-log sheet.

## USING A TIME-LOG SHEET

Transfer the top two priorities in each category—work, home, and personal—to a new sheet titled "TIME LOG." The one-page starter sheet can now be used to practice shooting "baskets" in the trash can, or you can keep the sheets in a manila folder or three-ring binder as a journal.

Include in your time-log sheet your feelings for the day, but state them positively. For example, I recently felt dumped on at work and at home. For my time-log sheet, I turned the sad and negative feeling into a positive statement: "I choose to spend time with people who appreciate me for who I am—I have a lot to offer."

Place the positive statement at the top of the sheet, on the left.

Jana, an Achieving Woman, is in customer service. Her one-page starter sheet gave her direction for the day. "The two most important things I could do at work today were to call the media for an event our firm was doing, and fill out activity sheets for two other clients."

Here's what Jana's time log looks like:

**TIME LOG**

May 15, 19__
Wednesday

Positive Comment: Things have a way of working out—stay positive.

| *Work:* | *Hours Spent* | *Completed* |
|---|---|---|
| Priority: Make calls to media | | |
| Priority: Prepare activity sheets for 2 clients | | |

| *Home:* | *Hours Spent* | *Completed* |
|---|---|---|
| Priority: Wash two loads of laundry | | |

Priority: Set dining-room table
for Sunday brunch

*Personal:*                              ***Hours Spent    Completed***
Priority: Take a hot bath to
relax tense shoulders
Priority: Read

As you can see, the time log, in one glance, starts the day
with a positive comment; allows you to set and follow up
on daily priorities; and lets you examine the time spent
at work, at home, and for personal interests. It clarifies
exactly why you don't have a spare minute, if that is the
case. You will notice lifestyle patterns developing. In addition, you can examine where your time-stress comes
from: work, home, or personal tasks. When you understand where the stress is, you then know where and how
to focus on changes.

When Jana studied the lifestyle patterns that emerged
from her time-log sheet, she found she completed home
projects more frequently than work projects. This knowledge gave Jana a place to focus on her time-stress.

Cathie, a Traditional Homemaker, analyzed her time
log and found she was spending too much time volunteering at the hospital. "I get such a good feeling spending
my time volunteering at the hospital. I saw why I didn't
have any time to do anything else after reviewing my time
log. I was spending 25 hours a week at the hospital. By
the time I came home, I was too tired to start any new projects, including making easy and healthy recipes. I was just
diagnosed anemic, and I need to learn new eating patterns and substitute foods that contain iron."

After looking through her time log, Lauren, a Transitional Woman, found she was spending too much time
at work and not enough time at home or on personal
activities. "I started a job that had seasonal peaks, during

which there would be longer hours. After a seven-month "seasonal peak," I knew something was very wrong. I had a long talk with my boss. He hired a part-time person to do the extra work. I now work longer hours only during March and December and have more time to do things at home and for me."

## USING A TASK SHEET

I've devised a task sheet to organize events, review follow-up, and account for completion. The task sheet is different from the time log; the task sheet lists all the activities that need to be done to achieve the priorities listed on the time-log sheet.

Jana's time log, for example, listed her two top work priorities as calling the media and preparing activity sheets for two clients. Her task sheet would list all the activities she has to do to complete her priorities. In other words, it would list the names and numbers of specific media people and any other information she would need to complete her activities.

Jana's task sheet might look something like this:

TASK SHEET
- 325-8990   Channel 29
- 845-7905   Channel 22
- 888-7854   Radio 1620
- 777-4567   Mercury Alert
- 753-4445   Bistro Hotel—Client 1
- Itinerary typed & faxed—Client 1
- Summary letter, Jason—Client 1
- Confirm carnival booths—Client 2
- Distribute press release—Client 2

When a task is completed, she simply puts a line through its dot. The task sheet breaks down priorities into simple activities, alleviates the stress that comes from worrying that you'll forget something, and gives you a feeling of accomplishment for the day.

## REVIEWING AND REARRANGING YOUR CALENDAR

Look at your month-at-a-glance calendar daily and rearrange appointments if necessary. This daily review is necessary because events arise unexpectedly, a task takes longer to do than anticipated, and so on.

Once you decide on a priority, guesstimate the time you need to complete it and add 30 minutes. This additional time allows you to complete your task without rushing, gives you downtime before starting a new project, allows for any unexpected interruptions, and gives you extra time to think of what to do if a problem arises.

Sandy, an Achieving Woman, says: "Daily, I would call my next appointment and tell them, 'I'm running 15 minutes late.' I now cushion my schedule by 15 minutes between all appointments, meetings, and projects I'm working on. I don't fall behind as much. Occasionally, when I do, I call my next appointment *ahead* of time to say I'm running behind."

Look at your calendar several times a day, if necessary, and rearrange meetings or appointments to get your top-priority tasks completed. One day, Jackie, a Transitional Woman, needed to complete an itemized budget for the manager of the department. "I looked at my calendar in the morning and needed to change some meetings so that I could complete the budget. I had made several of these appointments weeks earlier. But the budget took priority, so I canceled them. I have found that most people welcome the free time. I do keep high-priority appointments, though," says Jackie.

# USING LISTS

You are already aware of how helpful a grocery list can be. As a working woman, however, you can probably profit from expanding your use of lists. Consider how the following lists might help you be more efficient:

- Customer-satisfaction lists
- Client-file lists
- Lists for others
- Running lists
- Errand lists
- Gift lists
- Movie lists
- Outing lists

The sections that follow will discuss each type of list.

## Customer-Satisfaction Lists

This type of list is a great way to keep in touch with your client and prevent miscommunication before a problem exists. If the problem is already established, the list helps you bring satisfaction.

Start a customer-satisfaction list for each client. It may seem like a lot of additional work, but once it's in place it will help you reap large social and financial dividends.

If you give customers service and satisfaction, most will be loyal. Staying in contact is one way to maintain communication, improve customer relations, and prevent problems.

## Client-File Lists

Insert a sheet at the top of each client file. Even if you do not plan to work on that account, list the things that

you need to do for that account. Once they're written
down, you don't have to waste time on remembering them.
The additional plus: It takes the stress off you if you forget
what needs to be done.

## Lists for Others

I list everything that I want my secretary to do each day.
When she finishes a task, she puts a line through the num-
ber of the completed task. I have delegated the duties, but
I maintain control and accountability.

Why not use a list to delegate tasks to your house
helper? Whether your helper comes in once a week, once
a month, or not at all (I need to talk to you), start a running list of what needs to be done around the house. I
went to grab a pencil that slipped out of my hand under-
neath a couch pillow. In addition to the pencil, I found
stale popcorn! Vacuuming under the pillows became an
item on my household task list. Add items to your list as
you find things that need to be done around the house.
The list will keep growing, I guarantee it!

## Running Lists

A running list is one that you constantly add to. For example, a retail store would do well to use running lists for
special orders. Rather than take the time to place several
special orders per day, the retailer could add the orders
on the special-order form as they come in and place the
order once or twice weekly.

## Lists of Errands

An errand list might be a running list. List the errands
that need to be done and add to this list as you think of

more errands. Don't waste time running errands every day; do your errands once or twice weekly.

You will find that you will take care of several errands at one place. The 80-20 rule says that 80% of your errands will occur at 20% of stores. In other words, if you had a list of 10 items, chances are that eight of them can be completed at two different locations. By doing errands in batches, you will save time.

In addition, consider delivery service. The small delivery charge may be worth it.

You may want to keep a separate list for Saturday errands, those that can only be done on Saturday because of school or work interference. Examples include children's haircuts, clothes and shoe shopping, or extra fertilizer for the garden vegetables. As the week progresses, add errands to the Saturday list.

## Gift Lists

Keeping a running list for family members, friends, and associates who "have everything" is helpful. When you're with one of these people and they mention that they would like to have something, write it down on a legal pad titled "Gifts." When the special occasion arrives, you have the ideal gift—something they wanted.

## Movie Lists

It's Saturday night and you want to rent a movie, but it seems as if you've seen everything. Keep a running list of movies you didn't have time to see at the theater or a movie someone suggested that you think you would enjoy. You won't waste time or get frustrated next time you go to the video store.

## Outing Lists

Start a list of vacation ideas or ideas for local weekend travel. If you read about a place you would like to visit, write it down on your running list. Include names of hotels, phone numbers, and addresses. Susan, a friend, takes her children to a large city 120 miles away once a month. She keeps a running list of places to go. She and her children look forward to this minivacation. Their last trip consisted of a children's play and church carnival equipped with candy apples and face painting.

## USING LEGAL PADS

On what should you write all your lists? I suggest using a legal pad. I started using legal pads over ten years ago. It was the only neat, large, and organized bound paper in the office. I suggest to my clients that they bring several legal pads when they have an exhibit booth at a conference and when they take notes at seminars and workshops.

Venus, an Achieving Woman, owns a beauty spa. She rented an exhibit booth during a women's conference. "Over 1,200 women attended this conference. I had legal pads titled 'Makeovers,' 'SPCA Charity,' and 'Boyfriends and Husbands: Addresses.' I received hundreds of good leads."

Carrie, a Transitional Woman, is a voracious note taker. "I used to take notes on tiny scratch pads given out at seminars. I ended up turning the pages more than I took notes. Since then, I've discovered legal pads. I get a lot of information on each sheet and can take as many notes as I need. I've never gone through an entire legal pad at one seminar yet."

## Important Points to Remember

Write down what needs to be done; don't depend on your memory. Written lists save time and relieve stress. Start each day by writing down what you think needs to be done and why it needs to be done today. This one-page starter sheet helps you define your two daily top priorities in the areas of work, home, and personal tasks.

Develop your time-log sheet to help you complete your priorities. Write down the date; a positive statement reflecting what is happening in your life; two top priorities for work, home, and personal activities; and the hours spent on the tasks. Follow up on task completion. Analyze the sheet to determine the areas in which you are completing your tasks and the areas in which you are not. This will help you make lifestyle changes, if necessary.

The task sheet can organize and account for the completion of activities. The sheet deters procrastination and keeps you from feeling overwhelmed.

Use your month-at-a-glance calendar to plan each day. Change appointments and meetings, if necessary, to accommodate your top priorities.

Save time and ease stress. Write it down!

# 14

# The Telephone: Woman's Best, and Worst, Friend

___

Of all the conveniences brought to us by Alexander G. Bell, the telephone is the most likely to become a slave-master rather than a liberator. Computerized phones with automatic dialing and other tricks hardly compensate for habits that all but destroy our intended schedules.

For most of us, it's incoming rather than outgoing calls that need to be monitored. Obviously, a crackerjack secretary is the best solution to handling both trivial and critical calls. But for those of us who lack the luxury of a top-notch right hand, there are tactics that can eliminate the enormous number of woman-hours that are lost at the sound of the bell.

___

## Understanding Telephone Myths

Two myths about phones hamper the efficiency of most working women. The first involves the need to answer the phone; the second involves underestimating just how much time answering the phone may take.

## Myth 1: "It's My Job to Talk to Clients At Any Time"

"Every time I sit down to do something, the telephone rings and there goes my concentration," laments a busy stockbroker–working woman. "In particular I feel the need to accept all incoming calls." This is a frequent comment. "I'm here for my customers, so I need to accept calls."

Of course you must communicate with your clients. But thinking you must be available at all times is unreal·istic and will lead to poor time management. And, as this chapter will discuss later, the best path to communication may not be a telephone conversation.

Don't burden yourself with the perceived need to be always available. The fact is, clients don't expect you to be available every time they call. After all, how often do you reach your doctor or dentist on your first try? They almost always have to call you back. And that's exactly what you need to train your clients to expect. As long as you get back to clients the same day, most will be happy. In fact, when you call back, most people will appreciate that you are busy and keep the conversation short.

Ruthie, a sales rep, doesn't answer calls from 2 to 4 P.M. and from 7 to 9 P.M. When she's in the office during those hours, the secretary answers the phone and explains that Ruthie will call them back. At home, she turns on the answering machine. "My problem," she says, "is that I can't get the paperwork done if I'm constantly interrupted. I make errors."

If you're a Traditional Homemaker whose work is at home, freeing yourself from the perceived need to answer the phone can be just as practical for you as for the woman who works away from home. You cannot be available 24 hours a day, even to friends and family. If you provide a way for people to let you know they called and then return calls faithfully, no reasonable person can possibly object.

## Myth 2: Answering Takes Only a "Minute"

Consider the time it takes to get back into the concentration mode. When you start a project it takes a while to get warmed up and start the ideas flowing. A phone call interrupts this process completely. When you hang up, you must start the process all over again. Writers know that the first couple of pages never flow as easily as their later work. Any interruption means they lose about 30 minutes before they can regain their concentration. If you value your train of thought and your time, don't answer the phone!

## SETTING NEW RULES

Let your clients and friends know that you are available at a certain time each day, twice a week, or whatever you decide. Then make sure that you are available at that time.

During the time they are available, many women do busywork. They write thank-you letters, address envelopes, water and feed plants, get out client binders for future clients, set up appointments, read inspirational sayings, or catch up on business-related reading.

This system allows you to do many of those things you wouldn't get done otherwise, yet it keeps you away from tasks that require concentration. Serious work gets done during the nonphone times.

## MAKING CONNECTIONS

Now that you have learned a few ways to guard yourself from unwelcome telephone interruptions, let's look at a few ways to make the most of the telephone when its use is appropriate. As mentioned, high-quality communication—not constant access—is the goal.

## Provide a Means of Staying in Touch

You must provide your callers with a way of letting you know they need you.

This could mean investing in an answering machine or voice-mail system and asking all callers to leave a specific message. Janet says, "I have never liked answering machines, but I succumbed and bought a cheap one. Six months later it didn't work, and I bought an expensive one. It gave out in 12 months. I'm not hard on machines; I rewind, I punch the button to listen to messages, and that's it. But they all seem to know how I feel about them."

Many working women share this feeling, but a lot agree that, since they don't have a secretary, they need one of these machines. The stay-at-home woman finds them useful when they help her guard uninterrupted work time.

## Why Talk?

Think about your incoming or outgoing calls. Are most of them conversational? Or do you need specific information, such as a person's name, the name of a project, a confirmation, or something else?

Voice-mail industry leaders say that half of all business calls contain one-directional information. That is, someone tells another person something. In most cases, the two people don't even need to talk; one person must simply convey information.

Many people waste time because they become locked into the idea that they must speak directly to someone. If all you need to do is convey information, be creative in looking at the many ways you can do it. You can prepare a message that contains the information and leave it on an answering machine or voice-mail system. You can relay the message through a secretary or another third party. (Leaving messages with a third party works best when the third party knows who you are trying to communicate with and what you want to convey or need. Always let your "secretary" know if you are waiting for a specific person to call.) You can write the information down and mail it, fax it, or drop it off. You will find these hints elsewhere in this chapter, but they can save you so much time that they are worth repeating.

If all you need to do is receive information, let the information provider know how he or she can leave word for you. In your message, say what the best time to leave word is and the time by which you need the information.

## Choose the Best Times to Call Back

When do you find yourself least in the mood to schmooze, or chat, on the phone? Usually before lunch and before going home from the office. Therefore, I have found that the best times to call back and ensure a brief businesslike call are from 11:30 A.M. until noon and from 4:15 until 5:00 P.M.

## Make Cluster Calls

As suggested, you do not have to be on 24-hour call, as long as you return your calls in the same day. When you are ready to return calls, optimize your time by returning as many as you can at one time. I call this making cluster calls. You may choose, as I often do, to call back between 11:00 A.M. and noon and between 4:15 and 5:00 P.M.—times when people are most likely to keep conversations short.

I find that another productive time for cluster calling is during the noon hour. I stay in my office twice a week until 12:30 P.M., making calls. You will be amazed at how many people are in their offices at this time. Many of them stay in at noon so that they can get quiet work done. They want to keep their conversations short so they can get back to work.

Remember that cluster calling doesn't have to be an at-your-desk activity. Put spare moments to use by making calls wherever you happen to be. I clip phone messages to my calendar, which I take everywhere except dressy social functions. I keep two paper clips on the calendar at all times, just for holding messages. I place the most urgent message on top, and arrange the rest of the pile in the order of priority.

I return calls as I'm waiting for my car to be washed (my time is worth more than the $7 the wash costs, plus I can't reach the top of the van). I also make and return calls at the orthodontist's office when I'm waiting for one of my three children's wires to be replaced.

Another good place to make or return calls is at your client's office. You can find out who is trying to get you by phone, and your client gets a demonstration of your diligence in checking messages and your promptness in returning calls.

The pay phone outside the entrance of most libraries will help you make cluster calls. It's also close to the materials you might need for research.

When you get into the habit of clustering calls, you will notice phones in places you never saw them before. By using cluster calls to respond on the same day, working women can exhibit professionalism and alleviate stress.

## Prevent Telephone Tag

Telephone tag is an annoying two-person sport in which one person knowingly or unknowingly calls another person when he or she is unavailable and then the second person does the same thing to the first person. These two unavailable people leave a string of telephone messages for each other. The result is the waste of valuable time and, in some cases, a lost sale, a blown deadline, or a critical misunderstanding.

Shelly, a realtor, says: "When I first started in this business, I was constantly chasing people. After I lost a few clients, I developed a new system. Now, I leave phone numbers and times with the company secretary and on my voice mail, so people can reach me. I check for calls at my office at least once an hour, especially if I'm in escrow. You never know what can happen."

This section will present several ways to prevent telephone tag.

**Find Out When to Call**   Most days you have a natural rhythm in your schedule. You may find that you are usually in your office between 8:00 A.M. and 9:00 A.M. or between 1:30 P.M. and 2:45 P.M. Your clients' schedules have rhythms too. Ask your clients the best time to reach them, and mark it on your Rolodex file or phone file.

**Use the "Twice Then Send" Approach**   Leona has a full-time job and manages 33 rental units. She uses the "twice then send" approach. "When I call someone on the telephone two times and can't reach them, I send a note in the mail. They usually get it the next day. In the note I tell the person what I need and to call in the information to my office. . . . I save myself a lot of stress doing this. I'm just too busy to play telephone tag."

Don't forget that, in some cases, faxing a message may be more effective than mailing it or phoning it.

**Use Home Phones**   When I have difficulty reaching someone, I leave a message stating my home number and ask the person to call me at a specific time. I give a specific time so that the call does not interrupt our dinner hour or come so late that it will wake someone up.

The same goes for reaching the other person. I bring their home number home with me and call between 7 and 9 P.M. I often do this on Monday evenings, since this is the day I get most projects started.

**Stop to Visit**    I have several clients who work constantly with their clients—a salon owner, an attorney, a stockbroker, a realtor, and so forth. There is a very small chance of getting them on the phone when I need to speak to them. If I am in the area and have 5 to 10 minutes (that's approximately as long as a phone conversation would take), I stop and have a conversation face-to-face. This helps me stay in contact and be available for them, even though they have hectic schedules.

**Use a Third-Party Relay**    Often when I'm at a client's office or the doctor's office, I'll return a call. If I can't reach the person I need to speak to, I leave the number where I am. I ask the client's receptionist to call me at my office if someone calls back for me after I've gone. The receptionists don't seem to mind giving me a jingle and relaying the message. Most times I think they're a bit surprised and impressed at what I will do to eliminate telephone tag.

Women with children should realize that their kids can serve as third-party relays at home. Not only can they prevent telephone tag, but they can—like a secretary—create a positive impression for you and your business. All children should know how to conduct themselves responsibly on the telephone.

Don't make the mistake of thinking that clients won't call you at home. As Shelly says, "I do so many things with so many people I never know which number, home or office, they're going to call. It's really not their fault, because sometimes I'm at my home during the day (for lunch and sick children)." I asked Shelly at what age she thinks children are able to relay telephone messages accurately. "As soon as they know their letters and numbers," she said. "I instruct them to repeat the names and phone numbers just in case. I'm one of those who gets very annoyed when I don't have the right information. Having the kids repeat the phone numbers alleviates the problem."

**Schedule Regular Meetings**  A marketing specialist I know works with two graphic designers. Telephone contact proved so difficult that she decided to hold weekly meetings with each one. Says Sue, "I need to spin on a dime with my clients—that's one of the reasons they hire me. Setting up weekly meetings with these designers ensures that we don't play telephone tag."

Similarly, Tina, a sales rep, and her major supplier decided to play tennis together once a week. Afterwards, usually over iced tea, they talk business. This gives them time to order more inventory; change policies; talk about any problems; and basically, regroup. "My major supplier is only in town twice a week. This time together allows me to get some good prices and up-to-date information on our business trade locally and in other locations. I have a strong suspicion that this is why we have such a good relationship, and in my business, it makes the difference between making a good living and just a living."

## TEACHING YOUR SECRETARY TO RUN INTERFERENCE

This section is for that lucky working woman who has a secretary or answering service.

The secret to making the best use of a secretary is keeping in close contact several times a day. Alert the secretary to the phone calls you want to receive. Tell him or her when you can be reached in the office and what you want them to say when you are not available.

Remember that your secretary's way of receiving calls—what the secretary says as well as the tone of the

conversation—is extremely important. All incoming calls
must be received warmly and competently. The feeling the
secretary generates has a direct influence on how your
client perceives you as a person and as a professional.

Establish these three important procedures with your
secretary:

- If someone has tried a few times to call you, apologize for the inconvenience. At this point the secretary should tell the caller that his or her message
  will go on top of the pile, and the secretary should
  follow through by putting it there and bringing it
  to your attention.

- Never ask the name of a caller and then put him
  or her on hold. The caller may feel unimportant
  if the call does not get through immediately.

- Always use positive statements. Don't say "No, she's
  not in the office"; say "She's at a conference today.
  Is there anything I can help you with?" Another example is "She's out of the office until noon, but I
  can reach her in an emergency." Other possibilities
  are "She's out of town until Thursday, but she checks
  her messages twice a day" and "She'll be back in the
  office at 2:30 this afternoon." The caller perceives
  a positive statement as an offer of help, not a dead
  end.

Two other rules of telephone conduct are as important for you as they are for your secretary:

- Wear a smile when you pick up the phone.

- Identify yourself. Ask how you can help the caller
  and follow through.

Use the same approach when you work with an answering machine or voice mail. Smile, be positive, ask how
you can help, follow through, and stay in touch. Just as
you need to check in continually with your secretary, you
must continually check your machine and voice messages.

## IMPORTANT POINTS TO REMEMBER

The telephone can save you time, provided you are in control. It's OK not to be available for calls 24 hours a day; your real responsibilities are to provide a way for people to let you know they need you and to respond to messages on the same day they are left for you.

Remember that you may not necessarily have to talk to someone directly to get a job done. Let your contacts know how and when to leave word for you. If you're the one who needs to convey information, find out the best times and means for doing it.

To respond efficiently to messages, cluster your calls and make them at times and at places convenient to you. To prevent telephone tag, send your message by mail or fax after two tries, use home telephones, stop by, use a third-party relay, or schedule regular meetings.

The impression a client gains through telephone contact can have a powerful effect. Make sure anyone who answers your phone—you, an adult, or a child—can convey a warm, positive attitude and take messages accurately.

Remember, the telephone is there for your convenience. Use it wisely, and it will be your best ally.

# 15

# LET GINGER DO IT:
# THE GENTLE ART
# OF DELEGATION

---

No man is an island, and no woman can do it all herself. No matter how small your business or what position you may hold in an organization, knowing how and when to delegate responsibility is critical for growth and success.

Proper delegation can double a working woman's productivity, no matter where she is on the career ladder. She must divide those tasks that involve policy from those that involve the actual operation of the business. It is important to remember that effective delegation goes both up and down the business hierarchy.

This need to delegate also exists on the home front. Delegation at home allows the working woman to spend special time with "delegatees."

## UNDERSTANDING THE NEED FOR CONTROL

Most working women have an obsessive need to control every aspect of their work, home, and personal activities.

187

This need for control, which inhibits delegation, stems from two sources: fear and guilt.

## Expel Fear

The Traditional Woman feels she needs to control everything that goes on in the home, particularly, or she will lose her family unit. The Transitional Woman is busy juggling her life and, if one baton drops, she fears she will lose it all—work and family. The Achieving Woman feels that if she loses control at work, in particular, mistakes will be made and her credibility will suffer.

## Give Up Guilt

Many women place unreasonable demands on themselves because they are running from guilt. They feel guilty about not being perfect, about not being able to do everything, so they redouble their efforts in every area. They try to control things to make other people happy.

The cartoon strip "Cathy" shows how feeling guilty about having a career caused one woman to redouble her efforts at being the perfect dog owner—even when her trouble was far from justified. Cathy comes home to find that her dog, Electra, has savaged the house.

Electra! What happened in here??!

The mail is ripped up . . . the pillows are shredded . . .
half of a blue suede pump is buried in the plant!!

Oh, Electra . . .

. . . I was gone too long today! You must have been so
bored and lonely! Maybe you thought I wasn't coming back! You knew you did something bad, and you
got scared and did something even worse!

It was all my fault! I shouldn't have been gone so long!

I'll make you a special dinner! I'll get out all your
toys!! I'm so sorry my sweet, sensitive puppy!!
GUILT: Dog's best friend.

Cathy's response seems extreme, but is it any more so
than what real-life women put themselves through because
of guilt? Consider a few typical cases.

Clare, a Traditional Homemaker, says, "Since I had a
part-time job, I felt I needed to do everything. My children
were busy doing homework, and my husband worked hard
all day. I ran myself silly just keeping up with the housework and washing. Then one day my eleven-year-old asked
me to play catch, and I said I had to do the wash. He said,
'Mom, why do you spend more time washing than playing with me?' That gave me a clue as to how to solve the
problem. Both the eleven- and thirteen-year-old now help
me with the wash and ironing, and I spend more time with
them—including the time we spend together with the
wash. All along I thought I was making them happy."

Linda, a Transitional Woman, went back to work after
her first child was born. She worked part-time for a while,
but she needed two full-time paychecks to run the household. "I hated to leave my baby at the time. I would run
home at lunch and directly after work to see him. I didn't
want to miss any firsts. I came down with a series of colds
that just lingered on for eight weeks. My doctor said I had
to either quit work or calm down. I stayed at work because
I didn't have a choice. I finally trusted my sister-in-law with
the baby, and you know what? I didn't miss any firsts."

Lani, an Achieving Woman, did everything herself in
her small business—including activities such as typing,
accounting, and filing, which she could delegate to others.
"I did everything myself because I knew where everything
went and I could do it faster than someone else. The only
problem was that all that work was piling up. I had no
choice; I had to hire someone. I went through four temporary workers before I found a good one. I can still work

faster than she can, but now I'm getting my work done, with a lot less stress."

An alarming but real thought: Life would go on if you were not here!

---

## CULTIVATING THE HABIT OF DELEGATING

If the examples in this chapter have made you realize that you are obsessed with control, the time has come for you to learn the habit of delegating tasks to others. To do so, follow this four-step plan:

1. Decide what tasks you like to do.
2. Prioritize your tasks.
3. Double-check your priorities.
4. Ask for help.

### Decide What You Like to Do

To begin to understand what you like to do, think about all your activities in a general way. A great way to review everything you do is to think about your tasks as you walk, jog, or do other exercise. After you have thought about the matter for a while, sit down with a pencil and paper.

Divide a sheet of paper into three categories—one each for work, home, and personal tasks. By category, list all the tasks you do now. As you review each task, ask yourself: Does this activity uplift me, give me energy? If the answer is yes, then the activity is one you enjoy. Circle it in green.

Next decide which tasks you feel neutral about; circle them in yellow. The tasks that remain uncircled should be the tasks that you not only dislike but that drain you of energy; circle these in red.

Keep in mind that there is a difference between an activity that you simply don't like and an activity that drains you. I don't enjoy washing dishes, but the task doesn't drain my energy. I not only dislike ironing, I find that it exhausts me and makes me feel irritable. Filing papers and magazine articles also drains my energy, as does doing some types of errands.

Obviously, the tasks circled in red are strong candidates as jobs to be delegated to others.

## Prioritize Your Tasks

Decide which tasks—at work, at home, and in your personal life—are really priority tasks for you personally. If one or more people could do the job about as well as you could and in the time available, consider letting them do it.

Sheila, an office manager at a law firm, was involved in accounting, public relations, interviewing callers, and much more. "The partners and I got together and brainstormed what each person absolutely had to do to make the firm profitable and which items could be delegated to others in the office. We felt I had to write the checks and accept all telephone interviews. We decided that I would delegate all outgoing correspondence and the ordering of supplies. This is a painful process. I hate to give control to someone else who doesn't care as much as I do. We're planning to have these brainstorming meetings once a month. I'm sure I'll let go of more responsibility, a little at a time."

## Double-Check Your Priorities

The priority of a task may change from morning to afternoon. For example, if you find you are running late in completing a task and another activity needs to be completed by tomorrow, you may need to drop what you're doing and go to the task with the pressing deadline. Mary, an Achieving Woman, had three priority tasks on a recent day. She needed to develop budget strategies for two different clients, as well as make a presentation to a new client. "I didn't realize how much time I spent on one of my client's budgets. It was 2:00, and I didn't have my proposal ready. Since I had an early-morning appointment with my proposal client, I dropped the budgets until I finished the presentation proposal. I finished one budget by late afternoon and had to finish the other one after my morning meeting."

How does establishing priorities relate to delegating tasks? Remember Lani, the small-business owner, who put off hiring help because she knew she could do the work faster than someone else? Chances are that you, like Lani, will be able to do the job you delegate faster than the person you delegate it to. In addition, assigning and explaining the job will take time. If a task has priority—if it has a pressing deadline—then doing the job yourself makes sense from a time-management standpoint. Find another activity on your task list to assign to a helper.

## Ask for Help

Most women have a difficult time asking for help. We feel there must be something wrong with us if we have to delegate. After all, we're women; we can take care of *everything*.

Why do women have so much trouble asking for help? After many informal surveys, I have found five basic reasons:

- The fear of seeming incompetent
- A dislike of infringing on others' time
- The fear of rejection

- The belief that a job requires specific knowledge and experience
- An ego involvement with the task

Before looking at some ways to ask for help at the office and at home, let's look more closely at each of the reasons cited in the preceding list.

**The Fear of Seeming Incompetent**   Women may feel that if they ask for help, they admit to not being in control of work, home, or their personal lives. Whether they are in control is not the real issue. The issue is women's sensitivity to others' perceptions of their capacity to be in charge.

**A Dislike of Infringing**   Here is another case in which women show their sensitivity to others. They may not ask someone for help for fear that the other person will say yes even though he or she means no. Women, from their past experience, know yes-saying behavior better than most. Certainly you have said yes to something that takes your time when you really wanted to say no.

**The Fear of Rejection**   Women seem to have an innate fear of rejection. This may explain why most women dislike making "cold calls" and prefer making "warm calls"— calling on someone they have met previously. People tend to avoid behavior that causes them to fear negative consequences. Therefore, we do not ask for help in case someone says no.

**The Need for Specific Know-How**   Working women are intimately involved with their tasks at work, home, and in personal activities. They know—through hard work and experience—which systems work. Being confident in this knowledge sometimes distracts them from spending their time in more efficient ways. Women need to learn that, if they ask for help and the other person's process is different from theirs and the end result is the same, it's ok.

**Ego Involvement**   A specific task may embody a woman's femininity, productiveness, or some other characteristic intrinsic to her ego. As a result, it is difficult to let go of that task. Carrie, a Transitional Woman, loved making her children's school lunches. "I made sure they had lettuce in their sandwiches, fresh fruit, and fruit juice. The hours of my new job made it difficult for me to continue. My husband took over, and I don't feel their lunches are as nutritious now."

## SEEING WHAT'S POSSIBLE

Once you have discovered the freedom of asking for help, you will find yourself developing new ways to organize and manage tasks. Consider the creative approaches that Sydney and Karen developed. Sydney, a sales representative for a large corporation, says: "I hate to make confirmation calls. I asked my secretary to do this for me, and I proofread her letters. It works out well for both of us."

Karen, an Achieving Woman, started laundry-folding parties for her family on Mondays and Thursdays after dinner. "The entire family sits on the floor in the living room and plays word games as we fold. We actually have a good time. My six-year-old, who finds the matching socks, asked if we could play the game on Saturdays."

## ENJOYING THE BENEFITS

You may already have discovered a fringe benefit of learning to delegate work. In the process of distinguishing the tasks that drain you of energy, you also discovered the tasks that energize you. You can use this understanding to revitalize yourself regularly and in stressful times, when you especially need a lift.

Jenny, who writes nonfiction articles, told how she uses one of her revitalizing activities. "When I'm at a standstill with my writing or I just don't feel like writing yet, I'll go out in the garden and weed or pinch back my herbs. It gets me going again."

Karen, a medical transcriber, takes walks around the office building. "I take four or five walks each day. Before I started walking, I would straighten out desk drawers, straighten paper clips, and other piddly things. I spent too much time straightening. Walking is a good way to help me with my diet, too—I drink more water."

Susan, a Traditional Homemaker, plays piano when she needs to be re-energized. "I don't play too well, but well enough to play hit tunes. Playing piano is just enough to take my mind off worries."

Kathleen, a Transitional Woman, says: "I started taking walks with the family, including the dog, after dinner. We clear off the table but don't do the dishes until after our walk. It's a good way to get refocused with the family after being gone all day."

## PREVENTING A RELAPSE

Being obsessive about control is so much of a habit for most of us that we are all in danger of forgetting to ask for help. Three major symptoms can warn you that you are trying to do too much. These symptoms are procrastination, the feeling of burnout, and depression.

### Procrastination

We've all done it—put off something until later. Besides not getting done what needs to be done, procrastination leads to the feeling of being overwhelmed. We keep putting off tasks, and the pile of tasks mounts. This feeling paralyzes us from getting our work done.

## Burnout

The word *burnout* comes from mechanical engineering, where it referred to damage caused by improper use. If you have been using yourself improperly by not asking for help, you have no energy. You feel as though you can hardly move your body, and your mind is just as sluggish. Prioritizing becomes very difficult.

## Depression

Depression is characterized by a lack of energy and the feeling that nothing is worthwhile. Depression causes inactivity and moodiness, which reinforce the depression. The depressed person feels that work and life don't matter. If depression is chronic, the sufferer should seek help from a doctor, member of the clergy, or counselor. Counseling can help a depressed person make changes that will reflect his or her priorities and, in so doing, reinvest life with meaning.

If your procrastination, burnout, and depression are simple symptoms of overload, however, you can get yourself back on the track by delegating what you can and then doing something for *you*. The list that follows presents 15 ideas for self-nurturing:

- Take a morning off from work.
- Treat yourself to a Saturday at a salon.
- Tell the family you're off-duty for dinner and dishes for a couple of evenings.
- Cuddle up with a good book and a cup of herbal tea.

- Go out with a fun friend for the evening.
- Take a two-hour lunch occasionally.
- Have your makeup redone.
- Say no to any more responsibility.
- Treat yourself to a facial.
- Spend a long, leisurely time in a bath; light aromatic candles.
- Take off an hour early from work, tell the family you'll be home after 8 P.M., and do something fun.
- Spend an entire weekend doing things you enjoy—no cleaning or errands.
- Hire someone to clean, iron, and do a few errands twice a month.
- Look at your calendar ahead of time and reschedule appointments during a busy day or week.
- Save $10 a week for six months and take a trip out of town overnight.

You *deserve* to do any one or all of these stress-reducing activities. If you don't treat yourself well, how can you expect others to do so? Remember, procrastination, burnout, and depression take more time and money in the long run than any of the 15 ideas from the preceding list.

## IMPORTANT POINTS TO REMEMBER

Working women need to give up the obsessive need for control. The Traditional Homemaker feels she needs to control because she fears losing her family; the Transitional Woman, because she fears losing everything; and the Achieving Woman, because she fears losing credibility.

To discover the tasks you can delegate at work and at home, list all your activities, discover the ones that energize or drain you, double-check your priorities, and ask for help.

Be aware of three symptoms of trying to do too much: procrastination, burnout, and depression. To prevent these symptoms, delegate work and do something you enjoy. Whatever it takes, do it.

Not only do you deserve a life with less time-stress, but preventing overload is less costly—financially and mentally—than curing the symptoms it can cause.

# 16

# A SEVEN-LETTER WORD: WAITING

---

Traffic congestion, doctors' offices, ballet rehearsals, soccer practices, clients' reception rooms, and being put on hold. What do all of these activities have in common? The need to wait. Learning to use the valuable time spent waiting is essential to effective time management. Waiting time does not have to be wasted time.

The thing that often keeps women from making use of odd bits of time is the lack of a critical tool or information. They don't have an address, paper, or Aunt Sally's sizes, for example. This chapter will discuss how to organize the trunk of your car so that you always have what you need. The chapter will also present many ideas for discovering the productivity of waiting time.

## USING YOUR CAR AS AN OFFICE AND KITCHEN ON WHEELS

Susan is a full-time accountant and has two children, one who is on call as an actor in commercials. Susan carries a hip buzzer and takes a two-hour drive for each audition,

**199**

callback, and taping session. Susan's car trunk is as important as the engine. She says, "I pick Phil up from school,
and off we go. On several occasions, I have one or two
added outfits for him, depending on the type of audition.
He's dirty from school, so I have a hair dryer, underwear,
shoes, shirts, and pants in the trunk. He just dresses in
the back seat."

What about satisfying his hunger pangs? "I keep car-
ton drinks, granola bars, and other dry food in the car
trunk at all times. I found out the hard way not to use
canned drinks. I also keep a lot of educational tapes, music,
and stories in the trunk. One trip I get to choose what
we listen to, the next trip my son chooses. Sometimes I
bring my second son along. While Phil auditions, Brian
and I spend some quiet time together. I actually look forward to this, even though my friends think I'm nuts. Otherwise, I'd be cooking and cleaning the house. This way I
spend more time with my children."

Vera, an account representative, has three children in
orthodontics. "One child always seems to chew on something and messes up her braces and needs to go to the
doctor's office. Have you ever been inside an orthodon-
tist's office in the afternoon? There are so many kids. I
plan my child's appointment for early mornings, which
helps a great deal, but I still have to wait. I spend the time,
usually around 45 minutes to an hour, doing PR with a
client or nearby supplier. I keep several company coffee
cups in the car trunk. Our customers love them because
there is a different saying on each one.

"Lucky for me, the office of one of my suppliers is
nearby. I call him a couple of days before the orthodon-
tist's appointment so I can arrange to talk with him and
drop off another coffee cup. I'm convinced this is why we
have such a good working relationship."

Divide your car trunk in half. In one half, store work-
related equipment, such as the expanding file folders I'll
discuss next. In the other half, pack family-related neces-

sities. This division helps to keep the trunk organized and neat.

## Develop a Mobile Filing System

I suggest that my clients buy three small expanding file folders. They cost under $4 each and can be used year after year. These files are worth their weight in gold. Label your folder to divide it into several segments: a segment for thank-you cards, children's birthday cards, adult birthday cards, all-occasion cards, scissors, tape, ribbon, wrapping paper, paper clips, and anything else you deem important.

The second expanding file folder holds reading material. Index it by topic: romance, sex, career, hobby, finances, parenting, and so on.

The third folder contains the active list: names, addresses, phone numbers, and other important information about clients, babysitters, doctors, close friends, the cleaning lady, and your hair dresser, to name a few. As long as the active list is in your trunk, you'll never have to make an extra trip home or to the office to get basic information.

However, the folder should contain more than names, addresses, and phone and fax numbers. Using one 5 by 7 card for each client, write down the last contact, whether in writing or in person, that you had with each client. Use this information to check whether you sent the birthday card or whatever. Don't depend on your memory for everything. Also list what you gave the client, if anything, at your last visit.

Ann, an account executive for a stationery store, is rarely in her office. "I keep a filing box in the passenger's seat of my car and call clients on the road. I even fax information to them from someone else's office. I don't have a cellular phone, but I know the location of every good pay phone. When I first started I planned my calls before leaving the office. Well, I soon found that my planning was in vain. Many of my prospective and existing clients couldn't see me, or I had to change times and didn't have their numbers with me. Now that I've developed a system, I see more customers and fit in a little play time on the side."

Your mobile filing system allows you to call, fax, write, or visit any person you're actively involved with, so that waiting time turns into positive action.

## USING WAITING TIME

With your car properly equipped, you're ready to be constructive wherever you find yourself. One way to use waiting time to your advantage is to write thank-you notes.

### Write Thank-You Notes

Writing thank-you notes often ends up on the bottom of the working woman's priority list. Yet this is a fairly simple task in terms of brainpower and time. Nancy, who has four children, does a great deal of waiting, transporting, and waiting again. "People always ask how I find the time to send thank-yous. Little do they know that I wait a third of my day," laments Nancy. "If I'm waiting for my girls at ballet and there's a card shop near, I march straight over and buy some cards. This wait time is the only real peace and quiet I get, except when the babies are napping."

If you want to positively impress your friends, clients, suppliers, and babysitters, write thank-yous. It does not take much time to write a quick note, especially when you're waiting, and the effort reaps an abundance in return. Very few people take the time to thank someone for their time or efforts. But when you do, these people will continue to be helpful and save you time in the long run.

For example, I have taken the time to nurture my relationship with the staff in my children's orthodontists' office. As a result, the staff accommodates me by scheduling the children for late-afternoon appointments. The children rarely wait over 5 minutes to get in (the two orthodontists have over 3,000 patients).

At work, I have spent time nurturing my printer. As a result, I receive completed printing projects days earlier than I would otherwise.

I suggest that my clients write one thank-you note a day. Working women have more than one person to thank each day: There's the sitter, for going that extra mile; the grandparent who came to the rescue unexpectedly or expectedly; the significant other who helped in some way; the client who suggested your name as a speaker; the supplier who corrected a mistake; the media, for showing up at an event; the printer who produced your newsletter within two days; and the customer who brought in a new customer.

To be able to write notes "in the field," you must have cards on hand. Keep attractive cards, with the insides blank, in your car trunk. Second, as you think of the person you want to thank, congratulate, or send a note "just because," write his or her name and address on an envelope. Third, slip the card (unwritten) under the envelope flap. Carry the cards in your month-at-a-glance calendar. (Remember, you always bring your calendar everywhere except social events.) As you wait for someone to return a call or for lunch, a child, a doctor, or a client, fill in the card. Drop your cards in the mailbox on your trip home. Sending cards is a great marketing and customer-relations gesture. A person's gut reaction to a handwritten note is always surprise and then appreciation.

## Talk and Shop

Andrea owns a women's clothing store. She actively promotes her store while she waits at her children's tennis
events. "Recently, waiting for my boys to finish their tennis lesson, I struck up a conversation with the woman next
to me. The woman was very thin. She told me she had difficulty finding clothes in her size. She had been in my store
but couldn't find anything to fit. Well, something was
wrong because we specialize in small sizes. I apologized
for the lack of proper service and set up an appointment.
She is now one of my best customers. Plus, we're good
friends to boot."

My husband and I go out to dinner at a neighborhood
restaurant once a week. The restaurant is in a shopping
center. We put our names on the waiting list and then go
midweek grocery shopping for milk, orange juice, fruit,
and other basics.

## Buy Gifts

People get married, have babies, recover from surgery,
move out of town, get a year older, and celebrate Bar and
Bat Mitzvahs, to list a few. These events usually call for
gifts. While you're waiting for a child or client, get your
gift buying out of the way. Sue says, "Valentine's Day is
one of my favorite holidays. I have a Valentine's area in
my hall closet. The week before Valentine's, I wrap several
gifts and place them in the car trunk. This saves me from
rushing to buy gifts. Since they're already wrapped and
in the trunk, I get them to the right people on time. In
addition, I sometimes preorder candies and cookies and
have them delivered."

When it comes to gift buying, catalogues can be a great
help. In addition, you can do your catalogue browsing during waiting time. Getting your holiday shopping squared

away will probably be much more satisfying to you than leafing through the old sports magazines at the dentist's office. I keep no more than three catalogues. I ask my husband and children to look through them and initial the items they like. I do my holiday shopping two months before I need to. I also choose gifts for other family and friends this way. No long holiday lines to wait in.

Glenna, a full-time stockbroker, does her shopping when she's out of town for pleasure or on business. "It's about the only time I have to shop. If I see something at a good price, I'll buy two or three. That way, I have the gifts I need for a wedding, housewarming, or whatever. I take advantage of wedding registries. I order the gift by phone and dictate the card's message."

## Return Phone Calls

What happens when you're not in your office very often and you need to return ten calls per day between working, transporting children, fitting in errands, and housecleaning? Chapter 14 presented several ideas for using waiting time to place calls from pay phones, clients' offices, and doctors' offices.

Jennifer, involved in telemarketing for her company, spends her day on the phone. She returns calls by using home numbers after work. For example, if someone conducts a home business, she knows she can use the home phone number to reach her contact in the evening. "If I'm waiting for one of my children after work, I'll call the home numbers and usually reach the people I need to talk to. This works for me."

Marty, a pharmaceutical salesperson, calls on doctors. "They don't have much time to talk to me to begin with, and many times I have a certain time frame to return their calls—in between patients. I write the times next to my sales sheet and try to call them at those times. I might be

getting my hair cut and have to excuse myself for 5 minutes
so that I can reach the doctor at a specific time to either
set up an appointment or to drop off sample drugs."

## IMPORTANT POINTS TO REMEMBER

Waiting can be a positive opportunity for working women.
Turn your car trunk into an office-kitchen on wheels. In
one half, store work-related equipment; in the other, pack
family-related necessities. Develop a mobile filing system
using three expanding file folders. In the first, keep cards,
paper clips, and gift-wrapping equipment. In the second,
keep reading material, indexed by topic. In the third, file
names, addresses, and phone numbers of active clients and
important others.

Write thank-you notes to clients, suppliers, acquain-
tances, friends, and family. Keep cards with blank insides
(for handwritten comments) at your office and in your
car trunk.

Use waiting time to return phone calls. Use restaurants
and clients' offices to return calls away from your office.
There is only one of you—let everything else wait!

# 17

# I'M COMMITTED: BUT TO WHAT?

The combination of a woman's talents, special interests, and everyday responsibilities put a heavy burden on her to make choices. What happens when someone asks a working woman to participate on the Board of Directors, help her son's first-grade room mother, be the assistant coach of the soccer team, or simply make dinner for a friend who is coming home from the hospital? Overload!

Working women need to use and enjoy their talents rather than be burdened by them. They must learn to make the best choices at the moment and not commit to those activities that take away from their special interests. Women need to avoid the overcommitment crunch.

This chapter will discuss how to avoid overcommitment by making expedient choices that coincide with your personal values and how to keep a positive attitude in the midst of it all.

## CONSIDERING CHOICE

Life is a buffet of choices—some good for you, others not. Before examining the techniques of choice making,

consider three issues that women often forget in regard
to their choices: freedom, education, and priorities.

## Realize Your Freedom to Choose

Women have the freedom to make decisions and choices.
You can choose where you want to work, what interests
you will pursue, and which school programs you will participate in. Sometimes women forget they have this freedom and the fact that, sometimes, the freedom to choose
means the freedom to say no.

## Choose Education

The best choices are educated choices. Therefore, take
every opportunity you can to broaden yourself. In some
places you can complete your college degree from your
television set. Correspondence courses are another way
of furthering education. Take evening classes; attend informal discussions; or expand your outlook through library research, reading, and spending time with people
you think have something to teach you. As my dad frequently says, "No one can take away your education, and
only you can get it."

## Set Priorities

Therapists say that working women have too many choices
and that this situation causes us frustration and anxiety.
To avoid frustration and anxiety, you must decide what
is important to you at the moment and make the choices
that support what you think is important. In short, you
must set priorities. Setting priorities has been a focus
throughout this book, and it will be the key in implemen-
ting the choice-making techniques outlined in this chapter.

## Making the Choice
## to Avoid Overcommitment

To keep a rein on commitments, you must:

- Set priorities.
- Feel free to reschedule.
- Prepare.

### Set Priorities

What is important to you? Stop now and make a list. When someone asks you to do something, determine whether the job is in keeping with what's on your list. Say no to anything that isn't. Remember, however, that priorities change with your life stage. Daily priorities change as well.

Susan, a marketing director, says: "I plan every day, but I keep spontaneity at the forefront. My child is top priority, and I have to be able to drop things. I've always been a single mom. I divorced when I was pregnant with Misty. My daughter told me she was in a guitar recital the night before the program, and I had to reorganize the next day so I could be there. When I got there, the recital had been rescheduled for the following day.

"It's not unusual for me to schedule dinner meetings with clients at 7 P.M. so that dinner and homework are already done. My personal time is another major priority. My eight-year-old daughter goes to bed at 8 P.M. People ask me why bedtime is so early, particularly during the summer. I tell them I need quiet time for myself—I don't feel selfish. Occasionally, I leave Misty at the babysitter on Friday afternoon and pick her up Monday morning. We both seem to enjoy the time off from each other. The remainder of the week we spend special time together. I've set aside my real-estate career until she gets older.

Plus, I love my present job and don't feel the need to change now."

A college diploma is one of Stephanie's top priorities. "I worked out a schedule that lets me work full-time and go back to college. I should have my degree in five more years. If an activity doesn't bring me closer to finishing my degree or work, I say no."

Lani, a freelance bookkeeper, also follows through on her priorities. "My relationship with my husband is a top priority. I have learned over the years that when we're doing well together, the entire family does better. He called Wednesday afternoon, during tax season, and wanted to know if I could take Thursday off. It caught me off guard, but I rescheduled two appointments with clients (without telling them the reason). We had a great time together, and it gave me a much-needed breather."

Sue, a medical doctor, says "I prioritize *every day*. I try to limit the external pressures, including the number of committees I serve on. I avoid evening meetings, and I resigned as chief of staff at a local hospital when I became pregnant with my third child.

"I love my profession, but I made it a point to cut back. I leave my office between 4:00 or 4:30 P.M. and arrive home before my husband comes in at 6:30. Even though I work through lunch, I have fewer office hours than I used to, but I've made that choice. I figured this out after my second child was born. I was always rushing and found myself angry and stressed out. It took a real effort on my part to make the changes. If I have a patient who is extremely demanding, I'll refer them. They would be better served by someone else."

Susan, a school district accountant, is Jewish and feels strongly about Friday-night dinners. "I don't have to get up or leave early from work on Friday to prepare this meal. I buy the chicken, season it, and freeze it Thursday night. I put it in the crockpot when it's frozen Friday morning, and have the chicken ready by dinner. I make bread Thursday night, put it in a glass bowl, and store it in the refrigerator. I take it out in the morning and punch it down. Then I put plastic wrap around it and punch it down again at 4:00 P.M.—the kids throw the dough in the loaf pan and let it rise one more time. I enjoy cooking, and I'm not going to give it up Friday nights—the house smells good. The tone of the evening is special."

Nancy, a mother of four who suffers from rheumatoid arthritis, has adjusted her life to match her priorities. "Otherwise, I'd go nuts. I've set my priorities, and I'm not waiting for anything or anyone anymore. I used to wait to buy clothes or get a sitter. I got my guitar restrung—I was waiting on that, too. When the kids say, 'Mom, will you play "Chopsticks" with me?' I now say 'Yes' instead of 'Later.' I'm going on my cruise, even though my husband can't go. I guess I've made living right now a top priority."

## Feel Free to Reschedule

Most clients, family, and friends don't get upset with you if you need to reschedule a meeting, appointment, or an activity. A person usually gets upset when you do not call *ahead* to reschedule or you cancel at the last minute.

Susan has to reschedule her patients when there's an emergency at the hospital. "I've had to ask my patients if they could come in tomorrow morning. Most of them have not minded."

"I have so much going on at work," says Janet, "that I have to occasionally reschedule management meetings. I've learned that most people welcome the date change, because they are behind schedule as well."

Judy works full-time and does anything she can to prevent canceling a scheduled activity. "I hate to cancel something I committed to earlier. I have learned that I don't use the word *cancel*. To cancel something is 'flighty.'

I *reschedule.* I started doing this after someone I ad-
mired professionally rescheduled an appointment with
me twice."

## Prepare to Work Effectively

Once you have made a commitment, the best way to keep
it within the bounds of the schedule you've established
is to work effectively. This means approaching your work
efficiently as well as preparing a backup plan in case
something unexpected happens.

Candace, a staff manager, keeps files on her clients.
"I've worked out a system whereby each file has an 'action sheet.' That's the first thing you see when you open
the file. I list everything I have to do for this client and
check items off as I go along. It's a great way to delegate
some aspects of the job and still keep control."

"Because of my arthritis," says Nancy, "I double or
quadruple the recipe of everything I make. Yesterday, for
example, I couldn't cook. I went to our large freezer, a must,
and just warmed something up.

"I always quadruple the recipe for pancakes. The
children take the pancakes out of the freezer in the mornings and put them in the microwave. I know they've had
a good breakfast, and they're out the door."

Sometimes working effectively means not doing too
much work. Here's an idea for entertaining: Yes, go ahead
and entertain at your home if you like. But, make sure you
have at least one main dish and one hot appetizer
"catered." You can pick up these items at a local deli or
have a friend (who enjoys cooking) do it for a fee (offer
to watch her children one evening or weekend). You spend
a minimum of time in the kitchen and get applauded for
your delicious dinner. Hire your child or a high school
student to clean up. It's worth the $10.

## DEALING WITH OVERCOMMITMENT

Sometimes, despite our best efforts to avoid overcommitment, we find our calendars crammed and our energy
stretched to the breaking point. What then? This is the
time for another round of choice making—we must make
the right choice for that moment. This is also the time
for a sense of humor.

### *Make the Right Choice at the Moment*

You have your day planned, but you find yourself running
behind. You have much more to accomplish. What do you
do? You decide which client, activity, or meeting you need
to do *at this moment*. You must constantly ask yourself, What
is the most important thing I have to do *at this moment,*
and then do it. Reschedule or delegate everything else.
Susan says, "The key to managing my time is organization
and being able to change at a moment's notice. I've always
had that mind-set. It's simply survival. I grew up to be ac-
countable. I make choices—they may not be the right ones,
but I make them.

"If I'm hit with that tidal wave when all three kids ask
something of me, I try to meet the most necessary demands. If the others don't get done, they don't get done.
This is reality. The children have a right to make demands,
and I have the right to say yes or no."

In the course of re-evaluating your priorities on the
fly, you may discover that many of the activities that were
important to you in the past have outlived their usefulness.

Jennifer, for instance, always baked cookies for her
children's class events, even though she no longer enjoyed
it. For her, this habit had outlived its usefulness.

For four years Lori held Monday-morning meetings
with her staff. One of her employees suggested they meet

in the afternoon on Mondays, allowing everyone to get into the swing of things. "The afternoon meetings turned out to be extremely productive. I was setting the early meetings out of habit," Lori said, "not because they were productive. I don't hold early Monday-morning meetings anymore, even with suppliers. I need the time to get involved with what I'm doing."

Review the things you do each day at work, at home, and in your personal life. Eliminate activities that no longer seem important.

## Maintain a Sense of Humor

A sense of humor is a wonderful way to temper the feelings of anger, frustration, and anxiety that usually accompany overcommitment.

Janet, a single working mom, uses humor to keep her perspective. "Every night my daughter and I spend 20 to 30 minutes reading to each other. If she's angry with me or she's had a particularly difficult day, I'll read something humorous to her. When I'm having a tough day, I ask her to read to me—a motivational book or poems. It has a calming effect, and it keeps me in close contact with her."

Most "terrible" vacations; unbearable meetings; and uncomfortable work, home, and personal situations end up being humorous as time passes and the more you share them with others.

Susan, a medical doctor, knows the value of humor. "I try to put on a happy face and have a sense of humor. Let me give you an example. We were invited to another couple's house for Thanksgiving dinner. We received a call just before we sat down. The host, who's a surgeon, another guest who's a surgeon, and myself, the internist, had to leave the dinner. My husband ended up carving the dinner for himself and four children. It wasn't funny at the time, but that Thanksgiving has become a humorous family story."

Jeanie says: "I get so confused and overwhelmed by chaos. I have to keep things in control or I feel like I'm frozen in my footsteps. I've come up with OOPS—Organize, Organize again, Prepare, and Smile. The smiling part is probably the most important."

Humor is what saves Nancy on difficult days. "You have to have humor in life, especially with children. When I have absolutely had it, I hum the same Hawaiian song and I tell the kids I'm in Hawaii. It's my way of signaling that I need time alone. I used to get angry and yell. Now I use this approach, and the kids start laughing."

## PROTECTING YOURSELF FROM GOING CRAZY

This chapter has already discussed maintaining a sense of humor as one technique for dealing with overcommitment. There are other tips you can use to bolster your personal resilience in the face of overcommitment. Some involve developing a resilient attitude; others involve bolstering your outside resources. The list that follows summarizes these tips. (You'll note that maintaining a sense of humor is so important that it appears again.)

- Keep a positive attitude.
- Get enough sleep.
- Laugh a lot.
- Surround yourself with a support system.
- Maintain your perspective.
- Develop a peaceful refuge.

**Keep a Positive Attitude**  It takes more energy to deal with a negative frame of mind than with a positive one. When time-pressures occur, stay positive and do something about

them. My attorney friend takes 15 minutes each day to sit
quietly with her eyes shut. "I, personally, think of positive
things: a trip to the ocean, a healthy body, a positive out-
come in a trial . . . anything that makes me feel calm and
peaceful."

**Get Enough Sleep**   Studies show that a good night's sleep
helps the body act and the mind think effectively. How
many hours do you need to feel truly rested? Here's a rule
of thumb: If you feel tired first thing in the morning, then
set eight hours of sleep as a priority. It's a great way to
say no to evening meetings.

**Laugh a Lot**   The working women I interviewed who
have a good grip on their sanity laugh a lot. They're able
to laugh at their stressful lives and at the unbelievable
situations they find themselves in. I attended a funeral for
a 45-year-old man. His best friend told an off-color joke
at the service. About 80% of the people laughed, and the
other 20% didn't know how to respond. The best part was
that the widow was laughing.

**Surround Yourself with a Support System**   This is extremely important. I have seen dreams shattered and relationships broken because women have not developed a
support system. Nurture those relationships that make you
feel good, positive, and confident. Stay away from people
that make you feel inadequate and negative. It's hard to
do if these negative people are family members. But tell
them in a nondefensive way how their actions make you
feel. If this doesn't work, seek a clergyman or a therapist.
You cannot change anyone, but you *can* change your behavior and attitude. The change you make will change
others' behavior and attitude toward you. Stay positive,
laugh a lot, and be persistent. With these qualities your
odds will be better than those you'd find in Las Vegas.

**Maintain Perspective**   When time-pressures and events
start tumbling, maintain perspective. What is the *worst*

thing that could happen? If death is not on your list, relax. Remember, mistakes happen. It's what you *do* after the mistake that matters. If you have to reschedule appointments, then do it. If you have to be taken to the emergency room, you'd have to reschedule—why wait? Reschedule now.

**Develop a Peaceful Refuge**   Every working woman needs a place that's hers. This place makes her feel safe from everything else. For many women, it's their home. For others, it's one special room. Georgia bought a wicker love seat, lamp, and small table, and placed them in the corner of her bedroom. "It's my space," she says. "I go there to think, read, or just take a nap."

## IMPORTANT POINTS TO REMEMBER

You have many talents and special interests that increase the chance of your overcommitting yourself. To keep your commitments and responsibilities in check, do only those activities that are consistent with what you deem important.

As you go through your daily plans, keep a sense of humor. When situations become particularly difficult, look for the humor. Chances are good that you'll find a chuckle somewhere in the craziness.

Remember to reschedule, rather than cancel. Make the change as soon as you realize it needs to be done. The more notice you give, the better the result.

Prepare as much as you can at work, at home, and personally.

When you're feeling the time crunch, ask yourself: What is the most important thing I have to do *at this moment?* Then do it. Reschedule or delegate everything else. In addition, if you find yourself performing the same tasks and activities that you did several years ago, ask yourself: Has this activity outlived its usefulness?

There are six basic ways to protect yourself from going crazy: Keep a positive attitude, get enough sleep, laugh a lot, surround yourself with a support system, keep your perspective, and develop a peaceful refuge.

Priorities help you live the life you want. Choices keep you focused on your priorities.

# 18

# MEETINGS: RUNNING THEM AND ATTENDING THEM

---

Formal meetings are often the products of mindless routine and frequently get bogged down in a pattern of "touching mountaintops" rather than dealing with important issues. Such ineffectiveness wastes both time and money. Working women must learn to use meetings effectively, whether they are running them or attending them. This means knowing how to prepare for and contribute to meetings and how to communicate clearly. Clear communication calls for an understanding of body language—your own and that of others. Clear communication can save hours of apologies, frustration, wasted effort, and stress.

## KEEPING MEETINGS SHORT

Meetings play a vital part in business. However, it is important not to get "meetinged out." One way to prevent this is to keep all meetings to 55 minutes or less. If a therapist uses the 55-minute hour to discuss intimate details of feelings and interactions, then the working woman can accomplish a lot in the same amount of time.

A brainstorming meeting is the exception to the rule of the 55-minute meeting. Brainstorming meetings usually take several hours. By bouncing ideas back and forth, participants encourage spontaneity and creativity. Many companies, departments, associations, and groups brainstorm once or twice a year to foster new input, hash out problems, create new products or procedures, and plan.

As long as the purpose of the meeting is not brainstorming, you have a role—as the leader of the meeting or as a participant—in ensuring that it is short and effective.

## Control the Meeting as the Leader

Make the most of any meeting you are in charge of by following these suggestions:

- Distribute an agenda.
- Plan to start on the quarter hour.
- Start on time.
- Wait no longer than 10 minutes for participants.

### DISTRIBUTE AN AGENDA

An agenda includes the date and time of a scheduled meeting, the goal of the meeting, what will be discussed, and blank space for note taking. Every meeting should have an agenda, and the agenda should be distributed in advance, so participants can gather their thoughts and any other needed information.

The agenda is an active part in any meeting. It is not only important to follow along, but also to interact, whether you are the leader or a participant. As an idea comes to mind, write it down. If you object to something discussed, write down your feelings or any modification that you can suggest.

Keep clean copies of meeting agendas filed in a three-ring binder for easy reference and accountability. This prepares you to lead a future meeting or allows you to make a copy for an absent participant.

Mary, a business consultant, constantly uses agendas. "I wouldn't think of going to see a client and not have an agenda ready. This way, everyone knows the purpose of the meeting. I also have better control; I can move the meeting along if it goes off on a tangent. I constantly say, 'Let's move along to the next item.' I have even had meetings where I've written 'Brainstorming' under 'Agenda.' It gets the message across clearly and quickly."

### PLAN QUARTER-HOUR STARTS

Start meetings at 8:15 A.M. (if people attending are afternoon high-energy people) or 3:45 P.M. (for morning high-energy attendees). Starting at 8:15 in the morning allows you to get moving without wasting another 15 minutes waiting until 8:30. Starting at 3:45 means that participants will have enough time after the meeting to go back to their offices and organize for the next day. Sandy, an office manager, says: "I like having informational meetings at 3:45 in the afternoon. We never go past 4:30, and we get all the questions answered. I still have time to get back to my desk and make a few calls."

### START ON TIME

Start the meeting on time, even if not everyone has arrived. Some women feel uncomfortable starting with only half the members present. You may feel uneasy the first few times, but after that chances are good that your members will be there on schedule. Most of us do not like entering a room late.

## WAIT ONLY 10 MINUTES

If you schedule a meeting and no one shows, wait 10 minutes—that's all. You will show people that you are punctual and that you respect your time and want others to do the same. Again, this has to happen only once.

If the meeting is at a restaurant, ask the host or hostess to tell the latecomers that you left after waiting 10 minutes past the starting time.

Liza Jo, a sales rep, works her schedule around this 10-minute rule. "I don't care who it is. If they're more than 10 minutes late to meet me, I'm history. If they call to let me know they will be late, I either wait 10 minutes more or reschedule the appointment. This may seem a bit harsh, but time is one of my most valuable assets. The old saying 'Time is money' couldn't be truer in what I do. Since I've set this rule, I see nearly twice as many people a day as before. They know I act this way, and most of my customers are very punctual."

## *Control the Meeting as a Participant*

Keeping a meeting effective is easier if you're the leader than if you're a participant. However, there are ways you, as a participant, can help control the action.

- Ask for an agenda in advance and do your homework.
- Arrive early.
- Set time limits.
- Close out topics when closure is called for.
- Ask and answer questions.
- Volunteer to get information.
- Listen, listen, listen.
- Be aware of body language.
- Attend regular meetings faithfully.

By acting on the preceding suggestions, you will be noticed and respected as a meeting participant.

## ASK FOR AN AGENDA

Encourage the meeting leader to plan ahead by asking for an agenda before the meeting. Read the agenda and think about what you have to contribute to each item. If necessary, do a little research. Be prepared to cite resources, provide examples, or hand out articles that support your points.

## ARRIVE EARLY

Network with participants before the meeting. By chatting, prepare them for the topics that are to be discussed and get a feeling for the best way to present your ideas.

## SET A TIME LIMIT

You can't tell the boss when to end a meeting, but you can put a time limit in the leader's mind. When you come in, tell the leader that you have an important call coming at a specific time and ask if he or she thinks the meeting will be over by then. This keeps the leader in control but lets him or her know how much time you have.

If a meeting has gone past an hour, I have had good results by calling the leader afterward and expressing my concern. I explain my desire to stay for the entire meeting and outline my schedule constraints. Is it possible to keep the next meeting to an hour? The most common response is "My intent was to keep it to an hour. I know people are busy. I'll try to get the information presented within the hour next time. Thanks for calling."

## CLOSE OUT TOPICS

If someone goes on and on about a pet topic, sometimes you can close it out by summing up what's been said and then stating "If that issue has been addressed, perhaps we need to go on to something else."

Another way to provide closure on a topic is to suggest forming a task force. A task force can study all sides of an issue at length and make recommendations that will allow participants to settle the matter quickly at a future meeting.

### ASK AND ANSWER QUESTIONS

Experts say that most of the action in a typical meeting occurs in the last 20 minutes. To use meeting time to its fullest, ask and answer questions throughout the meeting; get the discussion going and keep it going. Someone has to start. And, chances are, the earlier you start discussion, the earlier the meeting will end.

### VOLUNTEER TO GET INFORMATION

During most meetings the participants decide to contact someone or do some research. Don't let action come to a standstill as everyone waits for a volunteer to do the job. Volunteer to do the job yourself. Volunteer to do only *one* thing at each meeting, however.

### LISTEN, LISTEN, LISTEN

By listening carefully, you will not waste the group's time by asking needless questions or introducing a topic that is not appropriate to the context. In addition, you will be able to tell when someone else goes off the track and tactfully bring the discussion back to where it belongs. Another benefit derived from listening carefully is that you can weigh all sides of an issue before making decisions. Your decisions will be better as a result.

### BE AWARE OF BODY LANGUAGE

You will learn more about body language later in this chapter. When you are in a meeting, remember to use body language that projects a positive attitude and an interest in what is happening. Use your knowledge of body language to detect the need for clarification or other action.

### ATTEND REGULARLY

If you keep up-to-date by attending all meetings faithfully, you will not have to ask for explanations and clarifications. In addition, you will establish your reputation as a conscientious professional.

## UNDERSTANDING BODY LANGUAGE

Consultants keep telling us that more time is lost through miscommunication than anything else. "In a normal two-person conversation the verbal components carry less than 35% of the social meaning of the situation while more than 65% is carried by nonverbal messages."[1]

Body language is more limited than verbal language and mainly consists of posture, clothing, facial expressions, eye contact, tone of voice, and movement. An understanding of nonverbal communication, or body language, can save time because it keeps you from misunderstanding what another person is trying to communicate. For example, when an angry person says "I'm not angry" but is so tense that he breaks his pencil, his movement should signal you to find out how he really feels. It's important to recognize inconsistency between what a person says and how he or she looks or behaves. Likewise, to maintain credibility, you need to be consistent in what you say and how you say it. Nowhere is this more important than in a meeting.

[1] McCroskey, J. C.; C. E. Larson; and M. L. Knapp. *Introduction to Interpersonal Communication.* Englewood Cliffs, NJ: Prentice-Hall, 1971.

The sections that follow will discuss body language cues to look for in yourself and others while at a meeting (or anywhere).

**Posture**   The way you sit or stand at a meeting says a great deal. Leaning toward the speaker and looking relaxed shows that you are interested in the topic. The opposite type of posture says you don't like or agree with what is being said or the way in which it is being communicated.

**Clothing**   Clean, neat, and color-coordinated clothes say you are professional and you take yourself seriously. Unpressed, sloppy, and stained clothes tell the other person you don't care.

**Facial Expression**   Smiling shows interest and respect. A frowning or poker face usually means you're uninterested in what the other person is saying.

**Eye Contact**   Of all the aspects of nonverbal communication, I see this one as the most important. Eye contact (looking into the other person's eyes) says you're interested and you're listening. Looking away or avoiding someone's eyes says you don't like him or her or what is being said; a lack of eye contact shows disinterest. I was once told that some world leaders wear dark glasses during negotiations so that their counterparts cannot see their pupils. Large pupils would tell the other side that they approved or liked an idea; small pupils would say the reverse. It would save a lot of time if no one could wear dark glasses at the world's negotiating tables.

**Tone of Voice**   A calm, soft tone of voice shows that your feelings on a topic will remain neutral, even though you may agree or disagree. The opposite is a sarcastic tone. Sarcasm is anger turned inward. Rather than letting someone know you're angry, for example, you poke at them with belittling remarks. Since women have learned not to show anger, women often use sarcasm.

**Gestures** Using your hands in describing an event or sharing ideas not only makes the information more interesting, but also helps bring in others' opinions. Crossed arms say you're keeping something away from the other person.

## *Clarify Inconsistency*

If the body language of someone at a meeting is inconsistent with what he or she is saying or acting, ask for clarification. You can do this during or after the meeting. A technique to use in follow-up calls is to ask the person to comment on the way he or she thought the meeting went or about the ideas presented. The other person will usually take it from there, and real feelings will become clear.

It takes far less time to clarify a discrepancy than it takes to undo the damage that miscommunication causes.

## IDENTIFYING THE TYPES OF MEETINGS

I have identified three basic types of meetings: planning meetings, action meetings, and social meetings. Each type has its place. You need to know why you're at a meeting and behave accordingly to maximize the benefits.

**Planning Meetings** This is where you brainstorm and share examples of other businesses that have used the ideas being considered. To maximize the benefits and save time at a planning meeting, do your homework. Prepare by asking for an agenda, and thinking about what you can contribute. Do any research that's called for.

**Action Meetings** This is the meeting where things get done. Research is completed and action tasks are determined. This is the time to say if something is going to work and the time to drop ideas that won't. Making realistic decisions now saves hours of thrashing through the same information later. A sublevel of the action meeting is the task force meeting. Be prepared to take action. The sole purpose of the task force is to save the group's time.

**Social Meetings**    This is a great place to network with old and new friends. Being able to see several people in one place saves time. Make the most of the opportunity by keeping in touch with as many attendees as you can. Use your name tag to your advantage: Rather than write your first and last name, write "Speedy Sam" if you've picked up the nickname because you work quickly. Or write "Nurturing Nancy," if you're a nurse, or "Slim Sandy" after losing 20 pounds. This is an excellent way to start conversation with new people. Tell yourself that you are going to meet three new people at the meeting and seat yourself next to someone you do not know. This is a great way to meet many new people in an hour. Stay positive and network!

## IMPORTANT POINTS TO REMEMBER

Meetings can be a problem, especially when you are not in charge, but they are essential and need to be controlled if you want to maximize efficiency and decrease the frustration caused by poor time management. If meeting participants do not arrive within 10 minutes after the scheduled start time, leave.

Most meetings do not have to go over 55 minutes. Save time by keeping a few guidelines in mind:

- Prepare or ask for an agenda.
- Arrive early.
- Start on time and set time limits.

- Feel free to start on the quarter hour.
- Ask and answer questions, provide closure, volunteer, and listen.
- Understand body language and constantly assess posture, clothing, facial expression, eye contact, tone of voice, and gestures. Ask for clarification if you see discrepancies between words, behavior, and body language.
- Identify the type of meeting; plan and act accordingly.

Make the most of your 55 minutes!

# 19

# THE END . . . OR THE BEGINNING

---

As you can probably see, achieving more in less time has a lot to do with deciding who you are in the first place.

If you are a Traditional Homemaker who is required to put a great deal of energy into a paying job, you will not be happy.

If you are a Transitional Woman who spends too much time at work, you are going to feel stress and guilt.

If you are an Achieving Woman who forces herself to emphasize the home, you will create frustration for yourself and feel overwhelmed.

Become aware of who you really are and how you really want to spend your time. I have found that any woman who is unhappy with what she is doing simply won't achieve what she wants.

---

## MAKING THE MOST OF TIME

I hope you have learned in reading this book that using your time well and being time-efficient depends on six major concepts:

• Making a commitment to be happy
• Discovering your own uniqueness
• Keeping the process in perspective
• Understanding that time is relative
• Staying focused but flexible
• Honoring your feelings

## Commit to Happiness

By making a commitment to be happy, you say that you have the right to be happy.

I believe true happiness is an inner feeling of calm and peace. It is the commitment to these feelings that will provide you with happiness.

Commitment is the reflection of your desires. If you desire to spend more time at home, then it is your commitment to this that will make it happen. If you desire to spend more time with special friends and family, then it is your commitment to this attitude that will bring it about.

Every 24 hours you spend brings you closer to who you are and what you want to accomplish in your life at work, at home, and personally. If you haven't begun to shift your time emphasis in proportion to your true character (Traditional Homemaker, Transitional Woman, Achieving Woman), I suggest you start doing it right now.

One word of warning: Do not try to do everything at once. If you are a Traditional Homemaker and are spending 60% of your time working, 30% of your time on your home, and 10% on personal time, you can't make the changes overnight. But, by making a commitment to start moving in that direction, you will get there. Cut down a little on the working time, stop taking work home, don't work overtime, or get a new job or shift to part-time work. Remember that using time correctly means first making a commitment to be happy.

## Discover Your Uniqueness

*Where Did the Time Go?* is about becoming aware of your own uniqueness. There is no limit to who you are and your special talents and interests. However, you cannot be everything to everyone at the same time. What I suggest is that you get in touch with your own uniqueness, priorities, and motivational attitudes.

By organizing your thoughts and attitudes into one of three motivational lifestyles (traditional, transitional, or achieving), you can make time work *for* you. You are unique. There are no two women alike. It is your own uniqueness that I want you to discover.

I want you to notice your uniqueness by thinking about goals and by *writing them down*. I want you to find what motivates you and why. Are you motivated to work part-time, or are you pressured into part-time work by cultural expectations and others' demands on you? Would you like to spend more time at work? Or would you like to spend more time on personal activities, such as reading, sports, gardening, or sewing? What are you doing now, and how do you *want* to spend your time *now?*

## Keep the Process in Perspective

Enjoy the process. Rather than looking at waiting time in the grocery store or on a child's playing field as annoying, think of it as time to read a magazine or a reason to slow down and take a few deep breaths. Or take the time to put your arm around your child and give him or her a hug and a loving smile.

The decisions you make, the way you spend your time, the motivations behind what you do are all part of the process. Yes, you have demands placed on you; yes, your life requires change at times; yes, your motivations and attitudes bring out your true feelings about time and self;

and yes, some days you get more curve balls thrown to you than average. But all of this helps you put your time emphasis and daily 24 hours into perspective.

I would like to share an excerpt from Leo Buscaglia's book *Living, Loving & Learning:*[1]

> Yesterday is gone, and there's nothing you can do about it. It's good, because it brought you to where you are right now. And in spite of what people have told you, this is a good place to be! But there's nothing you can do about yesterday, it isn't *real* anymore. And tomorrow? Tomorrow is a wonderful thing to dream about. It's marvelous to dream about tomorrow, but it isn't *real*. And if you spend your time dreaming about yesterday and tomorrow, you're going to miss what's happening to you and me *right now*. And that's the *real* reality, to be in touch.

I wish a very dear friend of mine, an Achieving Woman, would take Buscaglia's words to heart. She spends her time in the future, always working for the next challenge. She works on borrowed energy and seems to put in more and more time at work. She is looking for the challenge rather than enjoying the process. She is always pushing herself, without learning from each step. She slows down when her body forces her to take sick days. Her latest bout of antibiotics cost her $60 for 20 tablets.

## Understand That Time Is Relative

I know how busy you are and the demands and pressures you feel. But it is time to stop feeling guilty and start taking control. The only thing you really have is time and you. Everything else is relative. Time is relative. How you view time as well as spend it make the concept of time positive

[1]Buscaglia, Leo. *Living, Loving & Learning.* New York: Fawcett Book Group, 1985.

or negative. Your attitude about time can help you save
or waste this precious personal asset.

This is one reason why my priorities may be very different from yours right now. It also explains why our
priorities change over time, through life experiences and
age passages. You can decide what your most important
priorities are *right now* and develop an action plan.

The only person you can control is yourself. Therapists
tell us that we allow others to upset us, control us, or waste
our time. When we place the responsibility for our actions
directly on our shoulders, it becomes more difficult to say
"I have to do this because so-and-so says I have to." Rather,
it is more accurate to say "I have to do this because *I* need
or want to."

It is, indeed, a great personal victory to know that what
you do, in the 24 hours allotted to you each of your living
days, will bring you closer to your goals.


## Stay Focused But Flexible

Staying focused on goals means being willing to expend
energy to achieve them and being able to accept trade-offs.

I believe that, if you stay focused on something you
want, chances are good that your subconscious will work
toward making your goal happen. The other half of staying focused is staying flexible. Focus without flexibility is
similar to a rubber band stretched to its limit. Focus, by
itself, restricts your choices and may tax you beyond the
human capacity to respond.

Staying focused and flexible has saved my nerves as
well as my sanity in the last two weeks. I was at a conference
for a week. I spent most of my energy reworking this book,
rather than learning and experiencing the conference.
Upon my return, I lost my house helper and I had to make
an emergency office move because of remodeling. I moved
into temporary space, a rental house, that closes escrow

in four weeks. Unless I find permanent space in two weeks, I will not have an office address.

This is how I have handled this situation. I defined a positive mind-set by saying to myself, I feel grateful that I had the time set aside so that I could spend concentrated time working on this book. Then I gave each family member more household duties while the ironing stacks up (that is my additional duty). At the rental house, I shut the door to the bedroom with wall-to-wall stacks of papers. I called a commercial realtor as well as friends, searching for permanent office space. I contacted an answering service to answer my business calls, and my previous receptionist will keep my mail in his box until I find a permanent address.

As you work to stay focused but flexible, consider these ideas:

- To choose your own Personal Motivational Lifestyle is to reflect on your inner feelings—your happiness, fear, guilt, loss, and so on.

- To identify your primary time emphasis is to commit to a happy life.

- To avoid guilt is to balance, not juggle, your time and your life.

- To develop alternate plans is to gain self-esteem.

- To find the time for love is to feel and nurture the real you and accept your vulnerabilities.

- To negotiate flextime is to appreciate yourself as a worthwhile human being.

- To take control of your schedule is to take responsibility for your life.

- To spend time to save time is to recognize your own value.

- To develop a home office or start your own business is to accept your strengths and weaknesses.

- To organize your desk is to organize your thoughts.
- To make decisions, right or wrong, is to exercise your freedom.
- To clarify issues is to honor and trust your feelings and decisions.
- To control the telephone is to accept it as your business associate.
- To delegate is to trust in your ability to let go of control.
- To use waiting time is to enjoy the process on the way to your goals.
- To make a commitment is to focus your sights and expend your energy on personal priorities.
- To communicate clearly with others is to be accepting of others' differences.

## Honor Your Feelings

Trust your intuition and decisions. Only you can truly come up with the "right" decisions and plans for you. By trusting your feelings and decisions, you have choices. I want you to choose how you want to spend your time ... your life. You have the choice to view time as your ally or as your enemy. Only through choices do you really have freedom, the freedom to be who you want to be and the freedom to live the type of life you want. Fight for your freedom. Only if you are free can you truly make life happier for yourself and those around you.

It is time to get all your senses involved in your life: sight, sound, smell, taste, touch, as well as feelings. *Now* is the time to develop high-quality relationships.

The greatest gift you can give yourself is to honor your feelings and decisions. The greatest gift you can give the people you love is you. You don't want to wait ... you do not know when your 24-hour clock will stop ticking. You must keep time as your ally, so that your hopes and dreams become reality. These hopes and dreams not only make you a happier person, but they positively touch the lives of those close to you.

I am on your side. I have seen many women literally change their lives by using this or a similar system. My professional, home, and personal priorities are always changing, but I keep my focus on the concepts I've shared throughout this book. Now it's your turn. And remember, every step of the way, though I can't be there in person, I'll be there in spirit, cheering you on. So, to all of you, I wish the very best!

# INDEX